MANAGING TO GET THE JOB DONE

How To Make Sure Your Employees Are Ready, Willing, And Able To Succeed

PETER A. LAND

 Executive Enterprises • New York, New York

This publication is designed to provide accurate and authoritative information regarding its subject matter. It is sold with the understanding that the publisher is not engaged in rendering legal, accounting, or other professional service. If legal advice or other expert assistance is required, the services of a competent professional person should be sought.—*From a Declaration of Principles Jointly Adopted by a Committee of the American Bar Association and a Committee of Publishers.*

ISBN: 0-7816-0607-1

Library of Congress Catalog Card Number: 93-073468

Acknowledgments

Dr. Ken Blanchard, co-author of the book *The One-Minute Manager Builds High Performance Teams,* offers the following truism: "None of us is as smart as all of us"; and so it was with writing this book. I want to express a heartfelt thanks to a special team of friends and loved ones who helped proofread, edit, correct, and improve this text—Bill Land, Beth Land Cookston, Gail Kelley-Webb, Pam Traynor, Susan White, Jay McAuley, Dennis Daniels, Bill Weems, Bob McGuffee, Jr., Marian Parker, and Dr. Diane Rivers.

In every major project there is one pivotal decision that profoundly shapes the final outcome. When I asked Chapman Greer, one of the finest English teachers on the University of Alabama faculty, to edit my draft, she worked a small miracle. She taught me the discipline of thinking constantly of you, the reader. If you find this book is easy to read, she clearly gets the credit. Thank you, Chapman, for your tough love.

Dedication

To Liz, Beth and Steve — the family that makes being a husband and father such a blessing.

Table of Contents

This book will teach you how to manage to get the job done and to make sure your employees are ready, willing, and able to succeed. The ideas I'll share with you really work on the job; they help bring clarity and order to your days as a manager. They will help you to top performance—and you will have fun doing it.

Over the past several decades, there has developed a management subculture. Most managers are familiar with the latest buzzwords and concepts. If we all actually managed as well as we talked, there would be adequate goods and services at competitive prices so that everyone could enjoy the good life. Yet each year we lose untold billions of dollars in productivity and thousands of people die as a direct result of stress. Much of this stress is caused by managers and supervisors who may know *what* to do but who do not really know *how* to do it. On the positive side of the coin, we can realistically state that one of the greatest reducers of stress is effective management and supervision.

The purpose of this book is to help those of us in management (whose success is determined and measured by the efforts of others) actually learn to translate some of the proven management concepts and principles into powerful action. I've shared many of the thoughts in this book with thousands of managers from Russia to Europe to Australia during my career as a consultant, trainer, and speaker.

While putting this book together, I asked my friend, Gail Kelley-Webb, an outstanding management consultant from Niceville, Florida, to read it for content and concepts. She has convinced me that this book would be of great value not only to practicing managers, but also to the consultants and coaches who strive to help their clients succeed. She sees the ideas discussed to be a valuable guide and resource for professional organizational development and management consultants.

Being successful at anything requires hard work. However, the consequences which flow from success are the sense of pride, achievement, growth, self-worth, and yes, even **fun** that makes life worth living.

Organizations are alive; they are living, breathing things. They have their own unique personalities, which some folks label "corporate culture." To me, the term "corporate culture" conjures up dullish grey bureaucracies with written do's and don'ts, should's and should not's. I actually see a personality; I perceive a soul—I hear a heartbeat.

I once heard "wisdom" defined as the things you learn after you know it all. As someone who has devoted his past thirty years to the study of organizations, both at arm's length and at close range, I've developed a few insights which have helped me immeasurably to understand a wide range of organizations—from the Cub Scouts to major oil companies, from hospitals to military units, from churches to state governments, from the PTA to multinational corporations. My relationship with each has left me with a few gems of wisdom that make me look with great excitement to my next encounter.

In this book I will share these insights—gems—with managers and leaders in all walks of life. The lessons I've learned are immutable laws; they work every time. They have never failed me; they have been hammered out on the anvil of my own personal experience.

I have made many mistakes as a manager. I failed to achieve my objectives because I did not *apply* business principles properly. In a word, I either did not understand the principles enough to apply them or I rationalized my failure to use them by saying, "We're unique. Those techniques won't work here."

The joy of writing this book, and I hope the pleasure you may find in reading it, lies in sharing my (gems) with fellow leaders and managers. As a student and practitioner of management, I take joy in seeing this complex art being performed well. It warms my heart to visit strong, healthy, viable organizations pursuing their goals with vigor and determination.

This pen-to-paper project is a true labor of love. I love good leadership and management, and I feel a kinship with other professional managers who share my excitement. Together, we can help you unravel the mysteries of non-performance and move your organization closer to excellence.

The overall plan for this book comes from the title of a popular song from my youth, "I'm Ready, Willing, and Able." That title served to focus my attention on the three major inputs to effective performance; this book will explore what it really means to be Ready, Willing, and Able.

As a leader and manager, your major objective is organizational performance. All organizations exist to serve a few core values—their reason for being. I want to dispel a myth. For years we've heard a lot about "organizational performance," yet organizations do *not* perform; that's a myth. The truth is—*people* perform. It's really the salespeople, secretaries, and supervisors—plus everyone else in the organization doing their "thing"— who create what we label "organizational performance."

If we want our organizations to perform and achieve their goals, then we've got to get every single team member, from the secretaries to the CEO, doing his or her part—in concert. When everyone is singing off the same sheet of music, there results a harmony that enriches the lives of everyone involved.

Isn't it heavenly to dream of everyone doing his or her job properly? I imagine we would eventually become bored with the success. Just one day in the management trenches, however, clears our heads of such euphoria; a manager's daily diet is rife with problems, with people not doing their jobs properly.

I don't want this book to dwell on negative things; there's certainly enough bad news in the annals of management history. But if we are going to shine light in dark corners and correct the problems of non-performance, we must understand the real reasons why people fail to do their jobs properly.

WHY PEOPLE DON'T PERFORM

As I consult for a wide variety of organizations, I can usually group non-performance problems into four major categories: task interference, imbalance of consequences, lack of skill or knowledge, and lack of/or poor feedback.

The first major reason for performance problems is *task interference*. This problem category will be discussed fully in Chapter I, but for now, suffice it to say that task interference results when our employees do not have the resources they need to accomplish the task properly. I see a person as "ready" to get the job done when the necessary resources are available for use. Throughout this book, we'll let *resources* equal *readiness*.

In addition to task interference, *imbalance of consequences* affects performance. Did you know that everybody comes to work every day for *consequences*? Of course, two valued consequences are pay and benefits. But there are many other highly valued consequences present in the work place: recognition, praise, promotion, development, pride—the list is extensive.

There are also negative or feared consequences associated with jobs: termination, layoffs, discipline, a plethora of down-side consequences that most of us would rather avoid.

If we were asked to sort out the tangible consequences from the intangible, we would find that pay/benefits/perks are tangible, but most of the other consequences are intangible. Pride, recognition, and a sense of achievement are intangible, but they are real. In fact, in some organizations, the intangibles are valued more than money. And it is the intangible consequences that managers can control on a daily basis.

When people feel that the consequence system is not in the proper balance with respect to their value system, they become unwilling to work. We'll talk more about consequences and their impact on motivation in

Chapter II, but for now, let's link the terms *consequences* with *willingness*.

Another monster lurking in the shadows is *lack of skill or knowledge*. When we first see non-performance, we must address the initial question, "Are the skills in place?" If the answer to that question is "no," then we train against the deficit. In actuality, people do not do jobs—they do tasks. Since we work at the task level, we must train at the task level. So, we establish organized training programs to put the needed skills in place. We'll talk more about *how* to train effectively in Chapter III, but it's helpful to see the strong correlation between *education/training* and *ability*.

The final culprit in creating non-performance is *lack of or poor feedback*. Every healthy system needs feedback. Formal performance appraisal systems are basically designed to meet the feedback needs of everyone in the organization. This will be the topic of Chapter IV.

I have mixed feelings about performance appraisal systems. First, they are important and necessary for determining promotions, raises, long-term development, and so on. In many organizations, performance appraisal interviews are either done poorly or not at all. Often, in more mature organizations, performance appraisal is highly valued; the company as a whole reaps the benefits of this important management responsibility.

When some supervisors complete the annual performance appraisal interview, they often feel they have filled the "feedback square" for another year; but *effective* feedback is given at the task level, on a day-to-day basis. In Chapter II we'll discuss feedback as a consequence and its impact on the employee's willingness; in Chapter IV we will look more closely at the leader's responsibility and techniques to help you provide high-impact, balanced feedback to the people who value it the most—your followers.

We will devote Chapter V to tying all these concepts and skills into a coherent whole. We will see what happens when leaders and managers actually apply the skills needed to optimize and integrate Readiness, Willingness, and Ability to Achieve Performance—a formula for success.

Since I see the role of a leader and manager from both the perspectives of a hands-on manager and a management consultant/trainer, I've added a separate appendix dedicated to the professional trainer and those managers who do their own training. We'll share some ideas to help you motivate adult students in seminars so that they will benefit most from their training experiences.

Now that the stage is set, we are ready for Act I. The title of this story is *Managing To Get The Job Done*. Its purpose is to help you lead your organization to top performance —and have fun doing it. As the plot unfolds, you'll get to know the players—R, W, A and P—and the finely balanced interrelationship between them that must exist if we are to succeed as managers.

As we meet the characters in turn, uncertainty will give way to comfortable understanding. This understanding will lay the groundwork for a new and meaningful adventure into the fascinating world of management. When effective managers inspire people to work together in harmony, their profits, productivity, and people all grow. That's winning by every measure of merit.

If I were king, I'd issue a decree that everyone's chosen vocation must be rewarding and fulfilling—yes, even fun. Mastering the concepts and skills in this book will be rewarding, but actually applying them on the job will help you lead your organization to top performance, and you will have fun doing it.

NOTES ON INTRODUCTION

In the section Why People Don't Perform, we list the four major categories of non-performance as task interference, imbalance of consequences, lack of skill or knowledge, and lack of or poor feedback. These terms are not original with this author; they have appeared, in various forms, in management literature for many years. Ferdinand F. Fournies' excellent book *Coaching for Improved Work performance*, published by Van Nostrand Reinhold Company, Inc., 1978, relates these categories to effective coaching skills.

Chapter 1

R for Readiness

For you to manage to get the job done successfully, it helps to look at what any job is from a systems perspective. A job—any job, from that of secretary or technician up to that of CEO—is an array of tasks. When people come to work each day, they do not do their jobs; they perform tasks that make up those jobs. So the way to manage to get the job done successfully is to make sure that people are ready, willing, and able to perform each of their tasks.

Figure I-1 illustrates the process that goes on in the performance of any task in any job. The large circle in the center represents what is necessary to perform the task—the resources, consequences, and skills of the person. The arrows outside that core illustrate what the person does all day. The dynamic process of receiving inputs, adding value with skills and resources, and producing outputs is the essence of task performance.

This book focuses on that center circle. When people have the proper resources, they are *ready* to turn inputs into outputs effectively. When people are subject to motivating consequence, they are *willing* to do so. And when people have the appropriate skills, they are *able* to do so.

"R" stands for *Readiness*. For a person to be ready to succeed in performing a task, he or she must have the necessary *resources*—tools, equipment, space, etc.—needed to accomplish the task properly. This is how we prevent "task interference" problems. All jobs require resources such as tools, paper, typewriters, vehicles, phones, computers—the list is endless.

Let's apply this model to my administrative assistant, Pam. Her job requires that she accomplish a multitude of tasks. She does some tasks only once a year, e.g., taxes. Other tasks, such as typing and filing, she accom-

FIGURE I-1

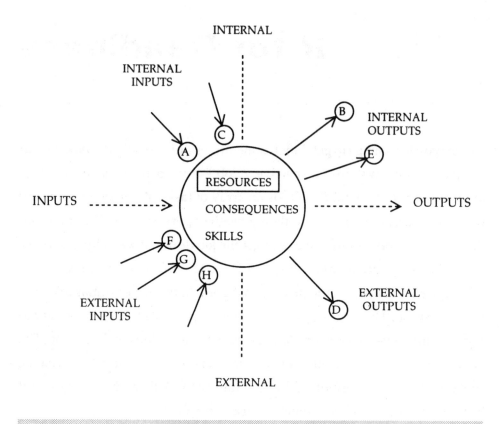

plishes daily. These tasks arise, as the diagram illustrates, from inputs to Pam's job. Some of these inputs arise internally from the organization, and some arise external to the organization. To perform these tasks, Pam needs functional office equipment.

Let's assume that I draft a letter by hand and give it to Pam to type. She gets an input which comes from within our company—she experiences an "internal input" (A). Her job is to use her skills and equipment to add value by typing the letter. Then she sends it to me as an "internal output" (B). I receive her internal output as an internal input. I add value by signing the letter; then I send it back to her. My internal output becomes another internal input to her (C). She makes an external output as she mails the letter (D) and an internal output as she places a copy in our files (E). Additionally, while we were involved in getting the letter mailed, her phone rang, which gave her an external input (F), the mail was delivered—external input (G), and she greeted a visitor—external input (H).

If you observe closely, you'll find that most jobs, whether sales, R & D, teaching, or manufacturing, can really be seen as a system of inputs, processes, and outputs. And you can specifically identify them, as we are doing with Pam's job.

TASK INTERFERENCE

Task interference performance problems are caused by breakdowns in the "resource" side of the equation; a lack of resources destroys readiness. As a management consultant, I often find task interference performance problems that are rooted in management's failure to provide the complete spectrum of resources—namely, time, tools, guidance, policies, and facilities. When you diagnose a performance problem caused by task interference, your first action should be to get the required resources. Task interference can be avoided by good supply discipline, inventory control, preventive maintenance, and back-up systems.

One day I rushed into my administrative assistant's office with a hurriedly drafted letter. "Pam, will you please type this letter? I need it by three o'clock." She had the skills, willingness, paper, and a functional computer. However, I had given her the draft at 2:58 p.m., and typing the letter was a ten-minute task. She experienced task interference because I failed to give her adequate time, which is an incompressible resource. I had to accept responsibility for her failure because I hadn't given her enough time.

A few weeks ago, I left her some draft letters to be typed while I was on a business trip to the West Coast. She had plenty of time, but I had done such a poor job of scrawling the letters that she couldn't read my handwriting—task interference strikes again. Now, we have expanded task interference to include "flawed inputs" and, as her supervisor, I was the culprit.

3

I recall vividly a large tire company in the Southeast. Throughout a five-state network of retail stores, they sold tires, shock absorbers, brakes, and other automotive supplies. One of the key tools of the mechanic, whose prime function is changing tires, is a pneumatic impact wrench used to remove and replace the lug nuts on a car's wheels. Someone in the company's corporate office decided to purchase their supply of impact wrenches from a cheaper source than they normally used, and he justified this decision with projected cost savings.

Over a period of months of using the cheaper wrenches throughout the Southeast, several auto accidents were caused when improperly tightened lug nuts came off recently serviced cars. The resulting lawsuits revealed that the failure mode of the cheaper wrenches was such that an inexperienced mechanic could not tell by "feel" that the nut was not tightened properly. The company stressed "fast service," which discouraged the employees from looking around the shop for the only torque wrench to check the correct torque on the lug nuts.

Bottom line—management had simply failed to provide the mechanics with the tools they needed to perform the task properly. As you may expect, the money the company had to pay in court greatly exceeded the cost of purchasing first-rate impact wrenches.

Most manufacturing operations are a network of subassembly feeder lines. For example, Departments A and B produce components which are sent to Department C for assembly. Department C's output becomes an input to Department D, and the process continues until the final product leaves the Shipping Department to the customer. Any breakdown in performance in any department creates task interference problems for every other department downstream.

A few years ago, I was called by a large manufacturing company which produces very fine wood products to investigate problems of personnel turnover, high training costs, absenteeism, and quality control. As I studied the company, I found one department which appeared to have stable inputs but produced unsatisfactory outputs in the form of substandard and/or delayed parts. The department also had high personnel turnover and excessive training costs.

The man at the helm of that particular department had been a reliable employee for twenty-eight years. He started as a carpenter's helper and had become a skilled craftsman who was dedicated to producing a quality product, thus reflecting his pride in the company and loyalty to management. This department head, whom I will call Joe, had never received any formal supervisory training, yet he was promoted to management as so many people are. He had proven himself with his technical skills and his undeniable devotion to the work ethic. When the previous department head announced his retirement, it appeared to everyone that Joe was the most likely replacement.

On the surface, there were no observable problems. But we must look more closely at the background and values of Joe to learn why he was faltering as a department head. His exposure to supervisory techniques had come from his former boss, whose leadership style had been shaped by his experiences during the 1940s when there was an abundance of labor and the jobs were not overly technical. If someone quit or was fired, a suitable replacement could be hired and quickly trained. When performance problems occurred, it was a safe bet that the reasons dealt primarily with motivation as opposed to skill or knowledge deficiencies. Many supervisors in the 1940s maintained production with a heavy-handed style; fear and public humiliation were used to keep the troops in line.

As I chatted with Joe, I learned that his former department head honestly felt that a chief should "chew out" errant employees in public so the others would learn from the mistake. Having been influenced by this leadership style, Joe adopted it as his own.

The problem was that this heavy-handed style has lost its effectiveness over the years; it simply will not work today. Education, job opportunities, competition for skilled labor in the market place, and many other factors make that style not only ineffective, but often counter-productive.

As I shared with Joe the task interference model, I asked, "What are your tools?"

"My tools are those lathes and saws," he replied proudly.

"Do you personally operate those lathes and saws?" I probed.

"Well, no, my people do that."

"Then those lathes are *their* tools. What are *your* tools?"

At that moment he had an "Ah-ha" experience.

"I guess *my* tools are my *people*," he said reflectively.

"Yes, Joe, trained and motivated employees are the major resource of all managers."

He interrupted enthusiastically, "I guess since I have personnel turnover triple the industry average, I'm giving myself task interference."

At that moment he "unfroze" and became one of my best clients. He wanted to learn everything about how to properly orient and train new employees, how to provide positive reinforcement, and how to impose tactful discipline in private. Almost immediately, the trends reversed. Today, he's an outstanding supervisor with all the positive management indicators to prove it—low turnover and high quality production at minimum cost. The department's morale has soared. They are now a close-knit team, doing the right things and doing things right.

We all know the critical importance of good customer service; a business's very existence is often determined by the quality of customer service it provides. However, if you focus on "internal" customers you can see that the internal outputs of one department in an organization are the internal inputs to the next department in the work flow. In other words, the departments that use our outputs are actually our "customers." We can contribute to their success if we do our job properly.

Let's review the bidding. Even though certain management techniques may have been effective at one time, they often lose impact as subtle changes creep into the work environment. Be sure you use today's skills today; this will help reduce task interference. I've found that well-managed organizations realize that "school is never out for the true professionals." An on-going program of management training and development keeps everyone's pencil sharp.

* * * * * *

As managers, one of our major tasks is to make decisions. Using the task interference model, we can consider our tools to include inputs from our staff in the form of advice and recommendations. We use our skills, judgment, tools, and staff inputs to make decisions which become our outputs.

I recall an experience which brought this principle home in a memorable way. During my Air Force career, I served as the Commander of Scott Air Force Base, Illinois. I had a staff of fifteen people reporting directly to me, with over one thousand five hundred people, both military and civilian, in the organization.

I had assembled my staff to discuss a labor relations problem; our goal was to make an appropriate decision about the particular issue at hand. As usual, I brought my biases and ego to work with me that day. After opening comments on the background of the problem, I began to present my biases. Soon there was absolutely no doubt in my subordinates' minds what I felt was the proper course of action. As we talked, I noticed one of our top labor lawyers, Capt. Lyn Dippold, becoming more and more uneasy.

After a while, I looked down at the end of the conference table and asked pointedly: "Lyn, you appear somewhat uncomfortable about the decision we're making. What do you think we should do?"

He blanched. He had two threatening choices: to take the safe path and agree with his boss or to take a risk and offer an opinion that was quite the opposite.

He took a deep breath and said, "Sir, may I speak frankly?"

I smiled and said, "You damned well better! That's why you were invited to this meeting."

He then proceeded to tactfully articulate an absolutely outstanding solution to the problem. When he finished, it was obvious to the casual observer that I had been pressuring my subordinates and taking my organization down a road that didn't turn.

There is a close parallel to the fairy tale of the emperor whose court magician conjured some beautiful new imaginary clothes. As the emperor walked proudly about in the nude, none of his subjects had the guts to tell him the truth, that he was naked. Captain Dippold had, in effect, told the emperor "you have no clothes." The young lawyer literally rescued us from calamity.

He finished sharing his wisdom and knowledge with us, and I felt embarrassed when I compared my solution with the one my subordinate had proposed. This was a moment of truth for me as the new leader of that organization. I could easily rescue my ego and impose my decision on the group or I could be honest.

"Lyn, that's a great plan; we'll do that," I said. "I admire you not only for your knowledge and expertise, but also for your professionalism. You came to this meeting with your homework done and then demonstrated the courage to make an honest contribution when it appeared risky. I see that as greater loyalty to our mission and organization than to your own personal security. It would be my pleasure to buy you lunch today."

The epilogue: I have developed an uncanny ability to take good information (inputs) and make poor decisions (outputs). However, I'm not smart enough to accept *poor* inputs (advice, recommendations) and make *good* decisions. I'm simply not that clever. If you're totally honest with the person in the mirror, I think you'll agree that you probably aren't either, and since getting high quality inputs (advice) from your subordinates is so crucial to the quality of your outputs (decisions), it would behoove us to sharpen our skills in this area.

Humor me for a few moments and accept the following premise. In the minds of your subordinates, there is a deep chasm between you and them. This "mental moat" is there because of the differences in pay, prestige, power, and perks. Despite the perceived closeness you think exists between you and them, the ditch is still there in their minds. The only way for them to come to you with valued, honest input is for you to build a bridge over which they will freely travel.

The key question is—how do you build a "mental" bridge across a chasm that you may not perceive yourself? You build this bridge through your actions as a sensitive listener, as someone who truly values the opinions and ideas of others, as someone who demonstrates openness.

Most people will not consciously put themselves in harm's way. If they see their career and promotion potential at risk for telling the boss what he or she may not want to hear, even the most loyal employees may conjure up a face-saving rationalization for remaining quiet or for following the party line.

I recall a company president who telephoned me because he was irritated that his people "won't talk to me." He wanted me to conduct a communications workshop to "shape them up."

After a frank discussion over lunch, I counselled him: "If your people fail to talk to you, it's not *their* fault—it's *your* fault." He understood; at the communications workshop he sat in the front row. He wanted to learn to build the mental bridge.

What are the timbers of this all-important bridge? First, we must listen. Oh, I know you've heard that *ad nauseam*, but I am talking about the skill of good listening as opposed to (1) "ho-hum listening," (2) "reply to refute listening," or (3) "look at your watch listening." Be wary of these and other tacky verbal and non-verbal signals we send to our people that say, "My body is here, but my mind is somewhere else."

I visited a client who complained of poor communications with his staff. As we approached his office, we passed the copy machine in the hall and he motioned me to a chair which was directly in front of his opened door. During our entire conversation, he must have glanced over my shoulder a dozen times to admire the secretaries who walked to and from the copy machine. Before I left, I told him how uncomfortable I felt competing with those lovely ladies for his undivided attention.

He was most appreciative of the feedback and moved the visitor's chair over by the window. In a subsequent conversation with him, he reported that communications with his staff had improved. Previously, he had sent non-verbal messages that he really did not want to listen.

In building our mental bridge, timber number one is, *Really listen*! Listen on all channels and send a strong message to your employees that the time you spend listening to them is very important—because it is! When you really listen to someone, there are two good things happening: First, you are learning and, second, you are stroking the person talking. You win in both cases. That's a real win-win.

Timber number two: *Ask questions skillfully and avoid hook questions*.[1] In a hook question, the answer is implied in the question. Say, you are called to your big boss' office to discuss a sensitive matter. Your boss has a strong bias toward a particular solution but says he wants your input and ideas. Your boss opens the discussion with, "Don't you think it would be best to....? or, "Everyone knows that alternative 'A' is best; what's your opinion?" Hook questions actually convey the message, "I don't really want your opinion unless it reinforces mine." It's far better to ask open, neutral questions like, "We are studying several alternative solutions to the problem; what are your thoughts on the matter?"

Timber number three is *Avoid groupthink* —the process that occurs when the group values harmony and cohesiveness to such a high degree that healthy dissent is suppressed. Irving L. Janis' excellent book, *Victims of Groupthink*, contains almost everything you ever wanted to know about this subtle group phenomenon.[2]

In classic groupthink, the group desires solidarity and unity so much that no one wants to ask the tough questions or to play the devil's advocate. In such an environment, decisions are made quickly and with great enthusiasm. However, history tells us that basically bad decisions can be the output. A kissing cousin to this classic groupthink is what may be called "power-driven" groupthink. The best way to understand this problem is to visualize this slightly exaggerated scene: The CEO is seated at the head of the conference table. To his left and right are executives #2 and #3 and the pecking order continues down to the gentleman seated at the far left corner at the opposite end of the table. Group norms dictate that the most junior employee sit there, looking forward to the day he or she can start "moving up the table" as his or her career develops.

Now that the stage is set, enter "power-driven groupthink." The CEO announces a proposed decision that he and executives #2 and #3 have developed. In order to get "input" from the staff, they have listed three alternatives—A, B, and C. As they present the alternatives, it's perfectly clear that choice "B" is their favorite; A and C are weak and are there primarily to make B look strong by comparison.

When the CEO opens the floor for discussion, the next most senior people "pick up the drift" and concur with choice B with few (if any) cosmetic changes. As the conversation develops, there is such a bow wave of views and opinions stated by the top brass that only the most foolhardy or independently wealthy junior employee would dare to offer an opposing view.

Groupthink is a snake in the grass. It appears as loyalty, agreement, consensus, and teamwork. When the CEO returns to his office, he honestly feels his team actively supports choice B. The good news is that choice B *may* be the best solution; the bad news is that it could be a disastrous decision lurking under the protective veneer of "groupthink."

Now that we have a clear picture of the wrong way to feign participation, consensus, and agreement, let's focus on the right way to get all these benefits without the down-side risk of "groupthink." First, you must create a climate of openness and trust by honoring those who speak frankly. I don't mean "frankness" to be interpreted as rudeness or arrogance. You should reinforce those people who demonstrate the ability to disagree without being disagreeable. Tact, diplomacy, sensitivity, and good manners are valuable behaviors around the conference table.

Second, if you bring a strong bias for a particular alternative to the meeting, I suggest you allow someone on your staff to present the problem to the group and lay out the alternatives. Select someone who has good presentation skills and preferably low power. He or she can present the clearest picture to your staff.

After the briefing is over, ask the lowest-ranking junior person this direct question—"What do you think is the best course of action and why?" If your "heavy hitters" attempt to interrupt before the junior member has an opportunity to speak his or her mind, sit on them! Their ideas will be backed up with power, and everyone below them at the table will have their candor and frankness blunted slightly. Don't let your senior people "poison the well."

After the lowest-ranking person has "spoken frankly," then work your way up the table. The next higher ranking person is not normally intimidated by comments from below, so you tend to get a valuable outpouring of fresh ideas; this resource is worth its weight in diamonds.

I must admit that I've chaired meetings when I walked into the room with a strong bias for my own pet solution. But when I've used the process described above, frequently I have learned just how flawed my original ideas were. As a decision maker, I looked wise and more credible because my ultimate decision was a combination of the best ideas of many bright people speaking frankly. One other great advantage to this process is that the people who have to implement the decision see it as *their* decision.

Each time Ken Blanchard and friends publish another of their *One-Minute Manager* books, they are packed with pithy one-liners that make loads of sense. I'm reminded of a quote from *The One-Minute Manager Builds High*

Performance Teams—"None of us is as smart as all of us."[3] The trick to generating no-nonsense inputs from your staff and getting smart decisions as a consistent output is to get "all of us" working the problem together.

Decision making is hard enough without self-defeating nuance and intrigue among the team members. Creating a viable up-channel communications network in the minds of your employees can pay big dividends. A few years ago, when I was the Director of Management Consultation for the United States Air Force, we had a team of consultants working with a B-52 bomber wing. The organization had been hassled for several months with aircraft scheduling problems.

As was our practice when visiting clients, our consultants were out in the organization chatting informally with the troops. One consultant was with the aircraft maintenance squadron on the flightline at 2:00 a.m. (Believe me, when you're standing in their work place in the middle of the night, you have instant credibility!) The consultant asked a classic question: "Sergeant Smith, if you had unlimited power and authority and could do one thing to make this a better squadron, what would you do?"

"I'd fix the aircraft scheduling problem that wastes our time and resources," he replied.

"Exactly how would you go about solving it?" the consultant asked.

The young Sergeant explained a very simple but effective solution to the problem. The consultant responded, "That sounds like a great solution. Do you mind if I pass that along to the Wing Commander?"

"No, I don't care," he muttered. "I'm scheduled to be reassigned soon."

In order to maintain confidentiality, the consultant asked, "Would you give me your permission to use your name?" "Well, I guess so."

At 9:00 a.m. that same morning, the consultant met with the Wing Commander for an update on the engagement. He shared the suggestion made by Sgt. Smith.

The consultant was taken aback by the Colonel's initial reaction. "Damnation! I wonder why that sergeant didn't tell us that six months ago? We could have saved a lot of valuable resources." After a moment's reflection, the Colonel answered his own question—"I guess it's because you took the trouble to *ask* him!"

That Commander fixed the scheduling problem before lunch. But he admitted he had learned a great lesson. "My people do not feel secure making suggestions, so they do what they're told." That day he set about the task of building the bridges of respect and trust over which Sgt. Smith and three-thousand fellow team members would travel with their ideas and suggestions.

Now that the idea of task interference is clear, we can also use the concept to our advantage in adversarial situations, if we so desire. One of the most gratifying jobs I held in my Air Force career was that of a Forward Air Controller in Viet Nam. My mission was to fly my OV-10 Bronco aircraft over the Ho Chi Minh Trail in Laos. It wasn't really a trail; it was a massive complex of roads, bridges, and tunnels that the North Vietnamese built in Laos to move guns, bullets, troops, and all manner of war material to the Viet Cong in South Vietnam.

My job was to find their trucks (big green bushes moving through the jungle) and direct air strikes on them to destroy the supplies before they reached their destination. I didn't realize it at the time, but I was in the "Task Interference Business." My job was to make the Viet Cong "run out of bullets." As a consultant, I've seen work stoppages and non-performance problems due to short-sighted purchasing, poor preventive maintenance, and weak supply discipline cause skilled and motivated employees to "run out of bullets."

Let's glance over our shoulder at the ideas we've discussed with respect to Readiness. As you recall, readiness means you have the resources—tools, equipment, supplies, space, time—and the best ideas from your people. Absence of or deficiencies in any of these factors creates task interference performance problems. Once we see the problem clearly, the solutions to task interference are not too difficult to implement.

14

NOTES ON CHAPTER I

1.   Langdon-Dahm, Martha. *Trade Secrets*. Dayton, Ohio. Learning Development Systems, Inc. 1986.

2.   Janis, Irving L. *Victims of Groupthink*. Boston, Massachusetts. Houghton Mifflin Company. 1972.

3.   Blanchard, Kenneth, Donald Carew, and Eunice Parisi-Carew. *The One-Minute Manager Builds High Performing Teams*. Escondido, California. Blanchard Training and Development, Inc. 1990.

W for Willingness

The "W" in our formula for success stands for *Willingness*. Once a person has the required resources and is ready, he or she must *want* to accomplish the task. And that motivation to succeed comes from desiring the *consequences* the person expects will result from performance. In this chapter we will focus on that part of the core section of the task performance diagram in **Figure II-1**.

ATTITUDE VS. BEHAVIOR

Before we plunge into the complexities of human behavior that calculate out to "Willingness," I want to clear the air on the difference between attitude and behavior. Our attitudes grow out of our values, our core of experiences, our goals—our total being. They are long in developing and slow to change save any Significant Emotional Events (S.E.E.), for example, being fired, getting divorced, suffering a major health setback, or losing a loved one. Our behavior, however, is basically what we do—how we act or perform. In most cases, our behavior is driven by our attitudes, but not always.

Let's assume that my values, background, experience, and biases produce in my mind a sexist attitude. My attitude is, "Women should not be in management; they should be secretaries and do all manner of low-paying 'women's work.'"

If women should "accidentally" reach responsible positions in my organization, my attitude could create a set of behaviors—such as not inviting them to the staff meetings, discounting their ideas, making them the object of sexist comments, and so on. Soon, the women in my group will say, "That man has the worst sexist attitude we've ever seen." Your attitudes reside in

17

FIGURE II-1

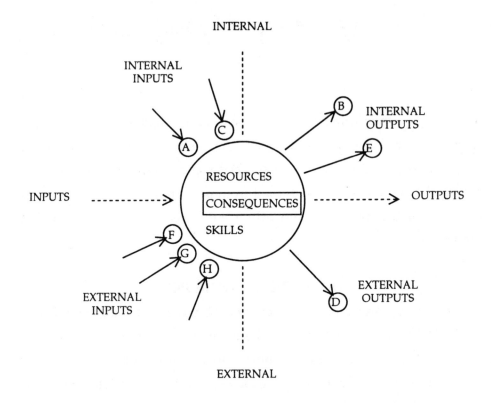

your brain. But your behavior is like your nose—it's there for everyone to see.

Let's look at take-two of the above scenario. Let's assume, despite my deep-seated sexist attitudes, that my behavior was different. All of the women who worked for me or with me constantly *saw* from me that I promoted them based upon potential; their opinions were valued; I listened—I mean really listened—to their ideas; I was fair and even-handed with both praise and punishment. I'll bet you anything you can eat that they would say, "He's a pretty good boss; I enjoy my job and I think I'll hang around until retirement."

18

What are they responding to—my attitude or my behavior? It doesn't take a rocket scientist to accept the fact that our people do not respond to attitudes—but only to our behavior. Successful managers and leaders are successful because of effective behavior—not necessarily because of their attitudes.

The following consulting experience indelibly etched the importance of this difference between attitudes and behavior into my brain: Several years ago, a major oil company decided to assign women to the off-shore production platforms in the Gulf of Mexico. For many years, the off-shore "Texas towers" had been male domains.

When the "good ole boys" who had long worked and supervised the off-shore crews learned of this new policy, many let their attitudes affect their behavior by stating vehemently, "I'll be damned if I'm having women on my crew; they shouldn't be out here."

Let's pause the tape here for a brief digression. There are two schools of thought about changing people's behavior. One approach is to first change their attitudes through counseling, encounter groups, and other long-term value-changing experiences. Another philosophy is quicker and cheaper but can be more traumatic—you change the consequences to such a point that they find it's in their best, short-term interest to change their behavior. Once they decide it is to their advantage to behave differently, then you train them as needed to put the new skills in place.

The oil company decided to follow the second approach in dealing with the supervisors' sexist attitudes and behavior. Management said, "If you refuse to supervise women properly on your crew, you will be fired."

The supervisors said: "I've only got a few years until retirement; I think I can work with women on my crew." That's when I was called upon to conduct a series of workshops on supervising women on the platforms.

The first thing out of my mouth in the workshop was: "Gentlemen, you supervise women just like you supervise men. Both sexes need to be adequately trained; they both need the required tools and resources; both

19

men and women need to be in the communication loop and listened to fairly. Just treat the women with the same respect and consideration you would want for yourself, and you shouldn't have too many problems getting them to help get the oil out of the Gulf." We devoted the next few days to learning and practicing the basic skills all supervisors need to effectively lead any employee—male or female.

Six months later, while conducting a follow-up visit on one of the off-shore platforms, I was chatting with one of the superintendents who had initially been the most vocal in his opposition to having women work off-shore. I commented, "John, I notice you have a female on your crew. How are things working out?"

His weather-beaten face broke into a warm smile. "Pete, I can't believe these words are coming out of my mouth—but Nancy is my best hand. She's bright, works hard, and knows this equipment out here better than anyone else. She gets along great with all the guys 'cause she does a great job. Yup, if I had about three more like Nancy I could let a few of the other 'slugs' go."

While this feels good on the surface, there's a deeper management truth buried here. Once the men decided it was in their best interests to accept the women and to supervise them properly, they paid close attention in our training sessions. They then applied the skills they had learned when they went back on the platform. They trained the women properly and treated them with respect. How did the women respond to their bosses' effective behavior? They performed superbly.

The good performance of the women became a new learning experience for the supervisors; they learned that their previous attitudes and values were no longer valid. They slowly replaced the old attitudes with newer and better supervisory attitudes. In fact, these new attitudes now drive their more productive and effective behavior, and will continue to do so until their retirement.

The most telling part of this story came as an afterthought. John made the following statement as I started to leave: "Pete, I guess I was wrong about my attitude concerning women on the platform. I think it's OK to have women on the platforms but only *if* they are like Nancy."

The consultant genes in me could not resist saying, "Yes, I agree that Nancy is a fine employee, but let's look more closely at your role in her success. You have been a fine supervisor; you provided her with excellent training, balanced feedback, listened to her, and provided the resources. She responded as most well-led employees will—she performed well. So I would like to modify your last statement. I think it's OK to have women on the platform but only *if* they have a supervisor like you!"

* * * * *

We are now delving into the most complex facet of human behavior— values, needs, desires, and wants. Let's group all these ideas under the general heading of motivation. The term motivation literally means "to move from within." The only *true* motivation is *self-motivation*.

I'm comfortable with the philosophy that the key to self-motivation is *consequences*. We all work for consequences; one we like periodically is a paycheck. Pay and benefits are positive, tangible, highly-valued consequences which tend to motivate us to get to work on time and do our thing. We are also motivated by positive, intangible consequences such as praise, recognition, professional growth, a sense of achievement, pride…the list is lengthy. In general, positive consequences are the best motivators, but we must take a balanced view and consider some negative consequences.

Termination notices and letters of reprimand are tangible, negative consequences which should result when we don't perform like "motivated" employees. Some negative intangible consequences which adversely affect our willingness and motivation include being ignored, "closed-door" decisions, prejudiced treatment, verbal abuse, a lack of deserved praise—yes, this list is lengthy, too.

Everyone has in his or her head a set of balance scales. As illustrated in **Figure II-2,** on one side, we put the value we place on our day-to-day efforts

FIGURE II-2

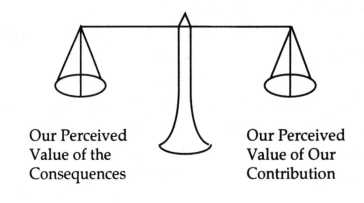

Our Perceived
Value of the
Consequences

Our Perceived
Value of Our
Contribution

which make up our contribution to our organization; on the opposite side, we place our perceived total value of the system of positive and negative consequences which flow to us as a result of these efforts.

If that mental balance produces the proper equilibrium *in our own value system*, then we will be willing (motivated) to maintain our efforts. However, if we calculate an imbalance of consequences, we will be unwilling to continue that relationship because we think we are giving much more to the organization than we are getting from the total consequence system.

This concept may appear somewhat simplistic on first blush, but it's not. The complicating factor is that this balance scale is formed by our personal values, needs, desires, our sense of equity and fair play.

I've seen many managers who feel that the consequences which flow to their workers are fair and reasonable, and they are baffled when their companies are hindered by poor morale (unwillingness) and thus low productivity. The CEO of a sales-oriented company conceived a campaign to stimulate the sales force. The top sales person was to receive an all-expense-paid trip to Bermuda, with spouse, to play golf on some of the finest courses in the world.

After ninety days, there were only minimal increases in sales; in fact, the

CEO commented that his sales team was "flat." I was asked to develop a sales training and motivation program to "jack-up" the sales force.

When I visited the sales department, I saw in the parking lot pick-up trucks with gun racks. The offices had hunting and fishing magazines everywhere. There were all manner of obvious signs which should, to anyone willing to listen, say "We are hunters and fishermen." I learned later that there was not a single golfer in the sales force.

Not only did the sales people see an imbalance of consequences, but it was also clear that the CEO did not know his people very well. You can probably guess who was the avid golfer in the organization; the CEO had offered a consequence (incentive) *he* valued.

I did not conduct any sales training; they were already skilled sales persons. All I did was give the CEO feedback on the perceived value of the golf trip to the outdoorsmen in his sales group. The next day there was an alternative prize—an all-expense-paid week-long hunting trip. Sales went through the roof. Obviously, the sales force needed only the proper incentive to produce record-breaking sales.

This concept is so important that I want to share with you another incident. Let's visit a large textile manufacturing company in the Southeast U.S., where everything had been going along fine. Then, over time, the good management, cheap labor, and other trademark elements of the Japanese began to beat the textile company to the marketplace. Soon, the American firm had fewer re-orders; cash flow problems made it difficult to make payroll. Now, the standard answer to payroll and overhead problems is to lay off people. When top management assembled in the board room to solve the problem, someone said, "Why don't we lay off some of our employees to keep overhead down?"

Someone else responded, "Wait, we have a large backlog of orders now. Why don't we wait until we ship the backlog and then lay off some of the employees?"

How long do you think it took those employees to figure out the consequences for being productive? As soon as that *consequence* appeared in the minds of four thousand employees, there were machines that didn't run, dyes that didn't match, slowdowns, sick-outs, and absenteeism. The firm had terrible productivity problems. So they called in a consultant and said, "We've got massive productivity problems, and we want you to set up a training program."

The consultant did a diagnosis and asked, "Did they perform well yesterday?"

They said, "Yes!"

The consultant asked, "Have you changed any equipment or procedures which would invalidate the skills in your work force?" They said, "No!"

He said, "Well, you don't have a training problem."

So the consultant went looking for something else that was "broken." He sat down with the people one-on-one and asked what was really going on. One guy said, "Hey, the name of the game here is 'Don't ship anything!' When the backlog goes, we go, so we do whatever we can to keep the backlog here and not get caught at it!"

The consultant went back to management and asked what they were *really* going to do; what's the big picture? They said, "What we're really going to do (but don't tell the employees) is lay off about two-thirds of those people, diversify, make a corporate investment, and compete in another niche of the market. Then we're going to bring about two-thirds of our employees back on the job. But don't tell them; it's a secret."

The consultant asked, "Why don't you tell them you are going to track productivity on the phase-down by unit level and the most productive workers get called back first?"

Now each worker was faced with six weeks or six months out of work. As if by magic, machines began to run; dyes began to match. They set productivity records on the phase-down. Why? Because the consequence system was in balance. Where? In their heads. It's not the consequence system in the manager's head that's important; it's the one that the employees think is important that controls their motivation.

I was consulting with a large retail floral company which had personnel turnover problems. Floral designers would take flowers, ribbon, and greenery and create value by arranging them artistically. They used about ten dollars' worth of material and sold the arrangements for $25. Their *skill* created the value. The company had 100 percent turnover in the floral design department; they required twenty designers on the staff and couldn't keep one a year.

My task was to improve the retention rate in the floral design department. I talked to the designers privately. Mary had been there eight months and had submitted her resignation. I asked her why she was leaving since she worked close to her home, her kids were in good schools, and the salary and benefit package was above the industry average.

As Mary and I walked to the floral design department, she asked me to look around and tell her what I saw. I said that it looked quite messy. She said, "Messy! This is a good day! We stand here ankle-deep in clippings and trash all day long, and it is just hard to be creative in such filth; it's simply a lousy place to work."

I said, "It can't be that difficult; why don't you talk to management about it?"

She said, "Well, we've talked to management about it, but we get a lot of rhetoric about their policies and rules that they've written down. We had one designer who really got upset about it, so they let her go; they said she had a bad attitude. The reason I submitted my resignation is that I've ruined three pairs of stockings this week, and I've had it!"

I went back to management and asked them what their plan was for cleaning up the place. The boss threw his shoulders back and said, "Oh, I have a plan, and it's even in writing! You see those drivers over there? Those drivers' job is to deliver the flower arrangements on their routes, and janitorial duties are in their position description. If they get back and get their vehicles serviced before 5:00, they sweep."

I asked, "What's the consequence for getting back early?" He had an "ah-ha" experience. He said, "You know, those guys never get back early. They always walk in here every day at one minute before 5:00, saying they'll catch it Monday, and Monday never comes!"

The drivers did not have a training problem; they knew how to sweep. They had an imbalance of consequences. All management had to do to fix that problem was to meet with those drivers, look again at the position description, and restate the policy and expectations. "You agreed to perform janitorial duties when you accepted the job." They agreed. "We're not going to pay you overtime for normal work, but we are going to assign specific areas of responsibility. Joe, this is your area and you work with these three designers, and so on. And the cleanest area gets another consequence— something that you, the drivers value, like tickets to a ball game or a free dinner with your wife. We're going to inspect your area periodically, and, of course, you don't go home until it's cleaned up at the close of each day's business."

As if by magic, that floral shop became a spotless place to work! I went back six months later for my routine follow-up, and I saw Mary; she was still there. I asked her how things were going and she said, "Great! Joe and I have this area here; we got the cleanest area last week. The other day, Joe came through here on his 2:00 run. As he walked by, I cut a piece of ribbon, and he caught it before it hit the floor!"

What do you think has happened to turnover in that company? It has dropped to virtually zero. In fact, they have people lining up to go to work there because it's a great place to work. The consequence system was put in balance. Where? In the employees' heads.

Another pearl in the string that helps create willingness is letting our employees know that their job is meaningful. We often fail to see the meaningfulness and importance of our employees' jobs because we compare *their* importance to *our* importance—we become the reference point. Invariably our subordinates come out second best.

The following story has had a profound impact on me towards insuring our employees that their jobs are meaningful to *them*. When I was in the Air Force, I worked with a chief master sergeant, Paul Smith. This is his story:

Paul married his high school sweetheart following graduation and joined the Air Force, which sent him to Lackland AFB, Texas, for basic training. Then he was sent to Keesler AFB in Mississippi for special clerk-typist training. While undergoing that course, he got a letter from his future boss, a staff sergeant, at a base in South Carolina.

The letter said, "Airman Smith, you are going to be on my staff. We perform clerical duties at an Air Force headquarters commanded by a two-star general."

When Paul got that letter, he became excited about his new job. He and his wife left for South Carolina, where they got settled in their quarters. On the assigned day, Paul reported for work.

His boss, the staff sergeant who had written him, explained his major duties. Part of his job was to turn in a brief report to a person two doors down the hall by 10 a.m. every day. That's all he needed to know; he could do that. Then the staff sergeant took Paul down the hall and introduced him to the people who received that report.

"Hi, Airman Smith, welcome to the organization. The information that you give us every day at 10 a.m. is important to us. We add some data to it and send it down to the command section every day by 11:00."

"Wow!" Paul said in amazement.

Then they took him to the command section and introduced him to the support staff who worked there. He looked into the executive office and there, behind a massive oak desk, was the two-star general, and behind the general hung an American flag.

Again, all Paul Smith could utter was, "Wow!"

They said, "Airman Smith, the information we get from you in your report goes on the flip chart we use when we brief the general. In fact, he makes decisions every day based on the information that comes from *your* desk."

A very motivated young airman went back to his desk to start his Air Force career. At only nineteen years of age and with one stripe on his sleeve, Paul sat at his desk and contemplated all that he had learned in the last twenty minutes. "You know, I'm surprised that this organization has run as long as it has without me!" he thought.

Paul Smith was motivated because he could see himself as a small, but important, piece of glass in the organizational mosaic, and he was willing from the very beginning to do his job. It wasn't the American flag, the pay, or the general officer; it was a staff sergeant, a first-line supervisor, who said, "Paul, what you do matters. You make an important contribution."

When the importance of his work clicked in Paul's mind, he decided he should get to work early, have those numbers checked and get them down the hall before 10 a.m. People at the office described Paul as a "highly motivated person."

Paul Smith became a chief master sergeant in minimum time, having become a supervisor very early in his career. The best promotions are those you get by being shoved up from below rather than pulled up from above; that's when people below you want you to do so well that they hit home runs for you every day.

The reason the people below Paul did so well and the reason he was promoted through the ranks in minimum time is that every person who worked for him during his twenty-four years of service got the same treatment he had gotten. Everyone who ever worked for Paul Smith knew he had an important job from the very beginning. That's how people get turned on; and, remember, employees don't turn over when they are turned on.

Effective managers keep in mind that they are there because the worker is there, not vice versa. Both sides have to win every day to make the system work. When people enjoy coming to work and feel appreciated and fulfilled, when they are earning a decent wage and learning in the process, when they have the skills and resources they need, and when management is out there every day trying to ensure that they can win, workers get turned on and they willingly climb into the organizational boat.

One of the most valued consequences to be found in the workplace is balanced feedback. This skill is so important that we are devoting Chapter IV to the leader's responsibility to provide feedback. However, since this chapter deals with willingness, I'll share a few examples of how positive feedback had a profound impact on a person's willingness and motivation.

FEEDBACK AND MOTIVATION

Write this in your "Book of Life": People tend to repeat behavior which is positively reinforced. I wish I had thought of that because it's profound. This is such a universal truth that I'm sure it could be deciphered from the inscriptions of caveman drawings from the Stone Age. The point to ponder is that it's true today and will be true into the next millennium.

As managers, we need a few golden nuggets on which to anchor our values and stabilize our behavior. Well, sink your teeth into that one; it's one of the immutable laws of human behavior.

Most folks believe, understand, and accept this dictum at the cognitive level, but many of those same folks either don't know *how* to provide positive reinforcement or just simply never get around to it—they say "I'm too busy." The following true story helps with the "how" phase of positive reinforcement.

Beth had done well in high school, but, upon entering college, she felt the normal apprehension as she went through in-processing and freshman orientation. There was a coffee scheduled for the parents, who were equally apprehensive. One of the college officials warmly welcomed the parents and spoke briefly about the facilities and programs that would "take good care of your child." In closing she said, "It usually helps with the adjustment if you will send your son or daughter a card or letter during their first few weeks."

One father took note; he was proud of his daughter and knew she would do well. He thought, "If sending a card to Beth will help her, I'm not too busy to do it." Have you noticed that we always have time for things we put first? He valued sending the card because Beth would value receiving it.

The next day he stopped by a drug store to select a card. He found several cheerful, up-beat cards that said, bottom line, "I love you." He bought six of them, all with different rhetoric and cartoons but the same message—"I love you," that is, *positive reinforcement*.

He addressed and stamped them, then tossed them, unsealed, into his briefcase. During the next week, as he travelled throughout the U.S. on business, each morning he would jot a brief note in a card, seal, and mail it at the hotel desk in his present city.

When he returned home from a week of hotels and airlines, his wife greeted him with a kiss and a "Guess what? Beth called and said, 'Dad sent me a card every day this week!'" She related proudly that Beth had really appreciated the thoughtfulness. She told her mother, "My roommates are really impressed that my Dad sent me a card every day!"

Beth graduated in the Spring of 1988 with a double major in math and physics and with top grades. She had worked hard and become a student leader. She had several excellent job offers and now holds a management position in a major corporation. Was her unquestionable success influenced by the fact that her dad sent her a card every single day for four years reinforcing the fact "I love you"? She thinks so.

FEEDBACK CONTRIBUTES TO ORGANIZATIONAL HEALTH

I was contacted by the administrator of a two-hundred-bed hospital. He was distraught over a serious rift between the local doctors and the nurses on his staff. To understand the problem, you should first appreciate the background factors.

As you know, most of the physicians you see in a hospital are not members of the hospital staff but refer their patients to that and other hospitals for treatment. Therefore, the patient care team is led by a physician who does not actually work for the hospital, although most patients think he or she does.

In this particular area, the average age of the doctors practicing medicine in the facility was fifty-five. When these doctors attended medical school, the average nurse had a two-year certificate and served as the primary link between the doctor and the hospital. The doctors believed the nurses should stand at the foot of the bed with a clipboard and say, "Yes, Doctor."

Conflict was rooted in different role expectations. The average nurse at this hospital was in her mid-thirties, had several years of experience, and had earned an undergraduate degree in nursing; many had Master's degrees. In recent years, society has seen nurses as very important members of the

30

patient care team with increasing responsibility; some nurses in America have been sued for malpractice.

One day a physician and a nurse were making rounds; he issued an order for a particular treatment. After leaving the patient's room, the nurse politely offered a suggestion she felt would benefit the patient. The physician snapped, "Listen, when you have an M.D. behind your name, I'll listen to your treatment recommendations; but until then, just shut up and write down my orders!"

Needless to say, the wounded nurse retreated to the nurses' lounge to vent her spleen to the others. The doctor complained to his fellow physicians and the administrator about the "arrogant nurses"; the problem began to fester.

After several more similarly unpleasant exchanges, the nurses began to hold group meetings to commiserate. Even the patients and their families could sense the tension that pervaded the facility.

The administrator called a meeting of the physicians and nurses in an attempt to resolve the conflict. All the nurses attended but only a handful of the more vocal physicians bothered to come. (Bear in mind that the administrator has little power or authority over an independent physician.)

The administrator allowed the two groups to sit on opposite sides of the conference table. His intentions were more noble than wise. He did not have the skills to conduct a conflict resolution session nor enough power to control the physicians.

In a matter of minutes, the situation deteriorated. The two groups shouted unpleasantries across the table; some combatants did not delete the expletive. In the days that followed, many nurses began to update their resumes.

When I arrived on the scene a few weeks later, I politely chided the administrator for not calling me *before* the cat-fight. We now had a long way to go to rebuild the team.

I met privately with several of the key physicians. They came to the meeting because they, too, did not enjoy the hostile climate; they knew the organization was "sick." As we talked, they all agreed that there were serious problems, but most felt the fault lay with the nurses. Fortunately, one of the senior physicians was an informal leader and sincerely wanted to make the team whole again.

I discussed the power of positive feedback but explained that the nurses actually have two major areas of expertise. The administrator could give them feedback on their scheduling, paperwork, and supervisory tasks, but only a physician could provide valued feedback on their medical duties. When I asked, "When was the last time you complimented a nurse on her medical skills?" an embarrassed silence filled the room. The senior physician finally replied, "I haven't done that in months; I think we all have done a rotten job of providing positive reinforcement."

I taught them how to give positive feedback and gave them a chance to practice; they did so reluctantly. One of the physicians was a woman who had recently completed medical school. She wanted everyone to be sure she was not mistaken for a nurse, so she was very cold and aloof with the nurses.

My visit took place in early December. During the Christmas holidays, when the hospital was on reduced staffing, the woman doctor was on call in the building. At 2:00 a.m., an elderly man in the intensive care unit coded (that's hospital talk for "died"). Lights began to flash; bells began to ring. The head nurse in Intensive Care paged the doctor—STAT, STAT! ("hurry, hurry!").

Since the doctor was in the coffee shop three floors below, it took her a few critical minutes to reach the ward. In the interim, the nurse had accomplished several key procedures to help revive the patient; in such a crisis seconds save lives. By the time the doctor arrived on the scene, the patient's heart had begun to beat properly; his vital signs were improving.

After the emergency had subsided, the doctor returned to her office. She jotted a brief note to the nurse and dropped it in the in-house distribution box. Two days later, the nurse opened the envelope:

"Dear Nurse Smith, I just wanted to let you know what a fine job you and your team did with Mr. Johnson. Your fast and accurate work saved his life. Thank you, Dr. Jones."

What do you think the nurse did when she read that note? She went to see the administrator, shut the door, and wept. "That's the nicest thing that's ever happened to me in my professional career." After she regained her composure, she went to thank the doctor; they had a meaningful conversation.

Word of the note soon spread throughout the hospital. People began to volunteer to work with the woman doctor. Other doctors began to notice she was "covered-up" with enthusiastic help.

One doctor commented in jest, "I wonder if she's paying them under the table." She said warmly, "No, I'm not paying them—I just thank them when they do a good job." I cannot describe the turn-around in that hospital. It soon became fashionable to ask instead of tell, to praise instead of punish.

When I checked with the administrator a few months later, he didn't have time to talk because he was in the midst of planning the first-ever hospital family picnic. They had a tremendous turn-out; nurses, techs, support personnel and—yes—doctors played softball, threw horseshoes, and shared the positive feelings about their teamwork.

Now that we have resources and are willing to perform, we must examine the third element in the success formula—ability.

Chapter 3

A for Ability

The "A" in our formula for success stands for *Ability*. Once a person has the required resources and consequences to be ready and willing, he or she must be able to accomplish the task. And that comes from the *skills* the person has. In this chapter we will focus on that part of the core section of the task performance diagram, shown in **Figure III-1**.

In setting the stage for what follows in this chapter, I want to clarify some concepts and terms, such as the subtle, yet important, difference between education and training. Education and training are first cousins in the same family, but there are some profound differences between these two concepts that, when not thoroughly understood, can and will create organizational performance problems.

In general, education is the transfer of concepts and principles; it usually takes place in an academic environment. The output is knowledge and understanding. In other words, the student can discuss the concept and expound upon it in a term paper or on a test.

Training, on the other hand, is the transfer of skills; it usually takes place in a work setting with the usual array of tools and equipment. The output of training is the ability to perform; you have not really been trained until you can actually *do* a task.

In the late 1950s, I attended Air Force pilot training. The mornings were spent in a classroom learning the concepts and principles of aerodynamics (education), but every afternoon, my instructor strapped my young body into a jet airplane where I was trained to actually fly that machine. After a few days of flight training with my instructor in the back seat, he said, "Pete, you are now ready to fly alone; take it up for a solo flight."

FIGURE III-1

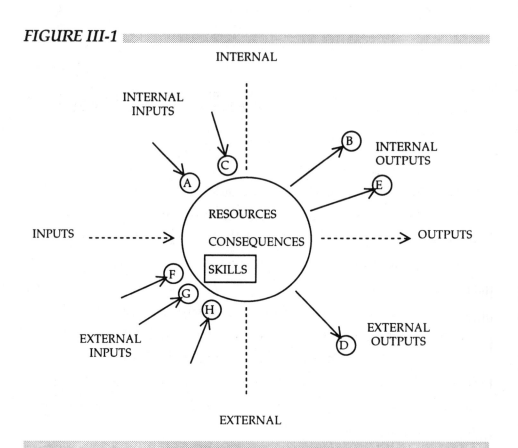

Let me assure you that your first solo flight brings home the significant differences between education and training. I had classmates who made 100 percent on every exam (education) but were eliminated from pilot training because they could never seem to master the skills needed to fly an airplane safely (training).

The point worth pondering from a management development perspective is that effective management and leadership is not what you *know*: it is what you *do*! Management, in general, and leadership, in particular, revolve around the actions of people. Your employees' behavior is directly related to your behavior, actions, and skills as a leader. Most people are unimpressed with a person's depth of management knowledge when he or she repeatedly does stupid things.

The flaw in our thinking stems from the insidious but often fallacious assumption that knowledge equals ability (skills). The history of management failures is rife with examples where the top salesperson was promoted to sales manager only to falter. The key managers were so impressed with the top salesperson's volume, production, work ethic, enthusiasm, and loyalty, that they assumed all these positive qualities of a good salesperson would, somehow, be mystically transformed into good leadership and management skills on the morning of the promotion. Sorry, folks, it just ain't so.

Fortunately, some such promotees have had the foresight to prepare themselves personally and privately for their first plunge into management, but far too many good salespeople—and engineers and accountants and technicians—find their first few months in management to be fraught with danger—they're flying solo in a jet plane without any prior training from an instructor pilot.

"A" STANDS FOR ABILITY

We hire incompetent people! Sounds a bit shocking, doesn't it? However, when someone is initially hired and reports to work on hour one, day one, he or she is not capable of performing any tasks which support the mission and objectives of the organization. We hire people for their potential, the future contributions we think they will make after they've been trained and motivated. As new hires enter the organization for the very first time, they are incompetent.

A new employee is a very fragile thing. How we handle him or her during the first few days, weeks, and months tends to cast the die for a successful or unsuccessful career.

The processes, systems, and techniques we use to orient and train these new employees are absolutely critical in determining how fast they become trained (competent) and how motivated (willing) they become to use those new skills to the best of their ability.

When we study the psychological make-up of a new employee, we find the following: they are very enthusiastic, thankful for being hired, anxious to make a good impression, willing to learn, and generally optimistic—that's the good news. Think how lucky organizations are to have that kind of raw material from which to build a strong, dedicated employee.

The bad news is that too many employees become unhappy, unmotivated, disloyal— and they depart. We label that process "personnel turnover." Turnover is one of the most costly and debilitating problems in organizations today; in the aggregate, it costs billions.

Allow me to perform an autopsy on this all too routine travesty and offer a few proven solutions to prevent it.

Figure III-2 depicts an employee's competence and productivity over time. Position "A" represents the employee's level of competence upon entering the organization on day one. He or she brings the aforementioned positive attributes to work that first day; however, just under the surface is low self-esteem. New employees are uncertain; they don't know even the most basic facts about the corporate culture; they know full well that they are

FIGURE III-2

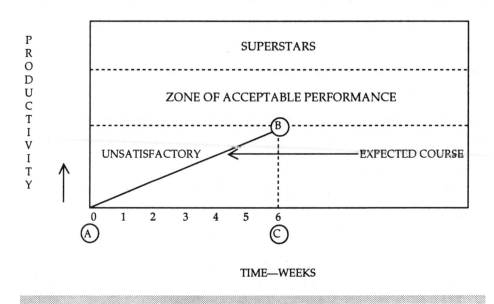

TIME—WEEKS

seen as the "new kids on the block" and are destined to do some "dumb things" and to ask a raft of "stupid questions" before they earn the respect of their co-workers and supervisors. If we were to take a new employee's "self-esteem temperature" the first day on the job it would, no doubt, be quite low; I've found this inevitable low self-esteem to be the biggest single problem in training new employees or long-time employees in new jobs. However, it is an established fact that people learn more, develop faster, and make fewer mistakes when their self-esteem is high.

Seems like a Catch 22. Try this: ask your new employee to report to your office at 8:00 a.m. on day one; you be there at 7:50 a.m. When she walks in at 8:00, (rest assured she will not be late the first day), she has presented you with a golden opportunity to deal with this low self-esteem issue. Say something like, "Good morning, Mary, I appreciate your getting here on time. I know dealing with new traffic patterns, unfamiliar parking, and such complications is not easy. We honor punctuality here; we're getting a good start on your orientation."

When you reflect on what you've done, this is what falls out. First, the new employee is nervous, unsure, apprehensive. The only task she was given was to be in your office by 8:00 a.m. She did it! Praise her tactfully and you'll boost her self-esteem significantly. It's easy to do; the hard part is realizing we have been getting to work routinely for years and have completely forgotten how confused we were on our very first day.

Next, let the new employee know immediately what to expect in the orientation and training program. Chart a clear course from "A" to "B" which represents the point at which we describe the employee as "trained" or competent to perform the job at a minimally acceptable level.

One key feature of this training program is an estimated completion date. In Figure III-2, I projected six weeks ("C") to complete the training program. In other words, I set a clock in the new employee's head that she will be at point "B" in six weeks. That's called creating clear expectations, a very important motivational ingredient.

The *truth* is that I personally expect to have the new employee at point "B₁" in *five* weeks—not six (see **Figure III-3**). I can expect such performance because I went to the trouble to check her references thoroughly; I studied our projected workload for the next few months; I have planned my work to include the quality time I'll need to get Mary trained in five weeks. But I keep this "real" date to myself.

The first few days are designed to get the newcomer comfortable in the industry, company, department, and office. This process is as old as Methuselah, so I won't devote any ink to it here.

After she has been "in-processed," you begin to introduce her to the "tools" of the job—computers, telephones, copiers, regulations, policies—*ad infinitum*. After you've familiarized her with the tools, she begins to use those tools to accomplish discrete, bite-sized tasks. Soon the tasks link together into more complex tasks, and finally, the tasks integrate into some coherent whole and we say with a drum roll and crash of cymbals, "You are now trained. Welcome to the ranks of the competent."

FIGURE III-3

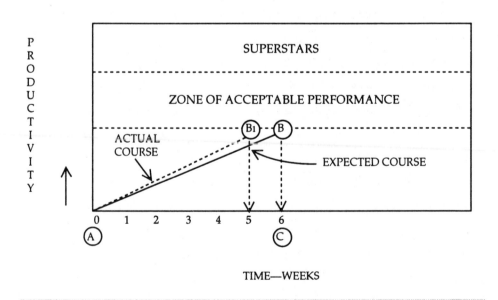

Let's go back and look closely at what's happening to Mary's self-esteem as we pursue the five-week program. She soon perceives that she's *ahead of schedule*—up goes her self-esteem.

The boost in self-esteem actually improves her ability to learn, which moves her along at an ever-increasing rate. This improved performance tends to boost her self-esteem even more, and the process continues to feed on itself.

The perceptions that invariably grow out of such positive and rewarding experiences are now deeply rooted in the new employee's value system:

1) I'm doing very well in this new job.
2) I enjoy coming to work.
3) My supervisor has a genuine desire to help me succeed.
4) I'm confident this early success portends a long-term successful career with this organization.
5) Yes, I clearly made the right decision in accepting this position. This is a great organization.
6) No, the other job offers I had (and still may have) are no longer of interest to me.

Upon reflection, we have created this situation by setting one set of expectations and then ensuring that the new employee exceeded them. We call that winning, and winning is fun.

Here's an ethical question: did we manipulate the new employee? The purist may argue yes; the pragmatist would say no. As a practicing pragmatist, I've never seen anyone who posted a resounding victory in the world of work and had fun doing it who felt they had been manipulated. Plan for success and you will succeed.

If you're not convinced that this system works, let me paint the dismal picture I see all too often. I'm going to over-state the case slightly to make the point. The new employee shows up at 8:00 a.m. and her boss is ten minutes late. The boss communicates, non-verbally if not verbally, that he has more important things to do than waste time with a "green bean." After a few perfunctory comments, the new employee gets shuffled off to another employee who is either unwilling, unable, or both, to show her the ropes: "I've got to go to staff meeting."

The new employee enters what is termed "incidental, informal, on-the-job training." It usually is formalized by the phrase "You work with Jack for a few days; he'll tell you what you need to know."

The organization has no training standards, no documentation that all the various tasks have been learned, no audit trail to establish accountability, no acknowledgment that the employee understands the task and, worst of all, no expectations of what success looks like (point B in five or six weeks). The untrained trainer says, "If you don't understand something, just ask." That sounds wonderful, but trust me, it's fraught with danger.

The new employee's self-esteem is already bouncing off rock bottom, so we say, "Ask if you don't understand." That's really stupid! First, she may not *know* enough to *know* she doesn't understand. Second, if she thinks she doesn't understand (blow number one to self-esteem), she's got to advertise that fact to the people she wants to impress the most by asking another stupid question (blow number two to self-esteem). So she doesn't ask and she makes a mistake because she didn't ask (blow number three to self-esteem). It doesn't take a very astute person to play this scene out. These blows create the following perceptions in the value system of the new employee:

1) I'm not doing very well in this new job.
2) I really don't enjoy coming to work.
3) My supervisor is always too busy to help me succeed.
4) I'm not sure I'm going to make it through the probation period.
5) No, I'm not too sure I made the right decision in accepting this job.
6) Yes, the other job offers I had are now of great interest to me. I

think I'll give Company X a call to see if that position is still available.

If Company X says yes, you've got personnel turnover—an organizational form of infant mortality. She leaves, and you start the whole mess again with another new employee. Overstated?—perhaps a tad. But it's worse when your employee calls Company X, finds the position is *not* available, and stays—all the while feeling trapped, cheated, and—yes—manipulated. While it's true that school is never out for the professional, this initial state of incompetence should have a defined window of time, after which the employee is characterized as "trained."

When I was a young Air Force officer, my boss, a salty old Colonel, assigned me the position of Wing Training Officer, which made me responsible for the training of our four-thousand military and civilian members. This was a bit unnerving since I had never had any experience in the training function. When I approached my boss to state my concern that I knew very little about the job, he responded with a statement that has subsequently shaped my values. This man's philosophy has been a guiding light in my efforts to develop the people who have worked for me throughout the years.

The Colonel said in essence: "Lieutenant, I can appreciate your apprehension, but a lack of knowledge is a *temporary* condition, and you have that job *permanently*. You see, two important factors in good performance are experience and knowledge. Experience is gained over time; it takes months and years to develop your core of experience. Knowledge, on the other hand, can be gained by study, hard work, asking questions—by hitting the books. The acquisition of knowledge is not so constrained by time; it's more a factor of our diligence, discipline, and dogged determination. I'll become your source of experience, but you have to work hard to gain the knowledge you'll need to do your job effectively."

As a consultant, I find management treating some employees as if their present level of knowledge was a constant, instead of a variable. We hear, "Jack can't do that," or "Susan is not capable of accomplishing that job." When I hear such comments, I hasten to add—"yet!"

When we accept the fact that people do not do jobs—they do tasks—we realize that people must be trained at the task level. It's far easier to see jobs as an array of tasks and establish a structured training program to transfer the skills, one task at a time.

Let's take a moment and review the basic skills you will need to learn and practice if you are going to be successful in management. In a classic article,[4] Dr. Robert L. Katz explains that there are only three levels of management in most organizations. The lowest level, supervisory management, is traditionally referred to as first-line supervision. The first-line supervisor normally directs the activities of the worker (non-managers). First-line supervisors usually have very little discretion on policy matters; they "execute" policy.

Believe it or not, first-line supervisors have the toughest job in management for three important reasons. First, they are usually promoted to management based upon their superior performance with their technical skills. They are chosen for supervision because they have demonstrated good work habits, loyalty to the organization, and the ability to get along with their boss and co-workers. We often make the fallacious leap in logic that such characteristics prepare employees to work effectively with the most complex system on earth—people. Second, first-line supervisors are normally not only our least experienced managers, but also receive the least supervisory training. And finally, the most complicating factor for first-line supervisors is that their various roles are unclear. Often, first-line supervisors are promoted from within; their subordinates were previously their peers and friends—their work group may also be their social group. For these reasons, their clout and credibility as a supervisor is often in question. First-line supervision is a hostile place to enter management. Unfortunately, many times we lose a fine technical employee and gain a weak supervisor.

44

Middle management is the next level Dr. Katz mentions. One of the distinguishing characteristics of middle managers is that they direct the efforts of other managers/supervisors; middle management starts with the boss of the first-line supervisor. Organizations have differing levels of middle management, depending upon how "tall" the organization is or how many "layers" it has.

As one moves up the layers of middle management, there are increases in pay, power, and perks, but the main difference is what I term "windows of discretion." The higher you go, the larger your window of discretion over policy matters.

The final level is top management. The line between middle management and top management is blurred—often it's in the eye of the beholder. Let me offer a personal guideline I use as a management consultant. When the President or CEO calls a meeting to discuss policy issues, the officers in that meeting are top management.

The windows of discretion at top management are very large indeed; the President/CEO has more discretion than anyone in the organization. In fact, the President/CEO has basically an unstructured role.

Several years ago I was addressing a group of top executives in Atlanta and said, "I haven't read your position descriptions but I can tell you what they say. You have three major responsibilities: 1) Operate at a profit, 2) Comply with the law, and 3) Guide your organization through the white-water rapids of competition." The group sighed in unison, "Amen."

Katz tells us that there are three skills needed to be successful in management. First is *technical skill*, which usually deals with things (tools, equipment, specific laws, sales, manufacturing, science, technology, etc.). Most managers enter an organization through some technical job.

Every organization has a focus of their technology. One of my clients is a major oil company. While standing on one of their off-shore production platforms in the Gulf of Mexico, I realized that the focus of their technology was on the tip of their drill bit, two-thousand feet below me, turning to the right. Everyone on that platform, and most of the employees "on the bank," blended their skills to make that drill-bit find crude oil faster, cheaper, "smarter" than the competition.

In addition to technical skill, I want to discuss *conceptual skill.* There are three components of conceptual skill. Long range/strategic planning is designed to answer the question, "What is the organization going to look like ten to fifteen years from today?" Organizational relationships answer the question, "How does my branch (department, division, office) fit into the next higher organizational entity?" The final segment of conceptual skill concerns corporate or organizational citizenship. This deals with the question, "How does our firm behave as a citizen in the community when it comes to the Blood Drive, EEO, pollution, and so on?" When you tie a string around these three concerns, you've got conceptual skills.

The final, and in my view the most important, skill is *human skill.* The definition of human skill appears innocuous enough, but as you think about it, the ideas, skills, and techniques involved are mind-boggling. "Human skill is defined as ability and judgment in working with and through people, including an understanding of motivation and the application of effective leadership."[5]

You see from **Figure III-4** that first-line supervisors must be well-grounded technically, for it is the first-line supervisor who must train, guide, motivate, even inspire the technical workforce. First-line supervisors simply must keep their technical "pencils sharp." We also see that first-line supervisors need at least an appreciation for the conceptual issues.

We note that middle managers require a balance of both technical and conceptual skills. Finally, we see that top executives are not valued for their technical skill so much as for their ability to deal with the conceptual and human issues. Recall what I stated in the Introduction: Top executives should have broad technical *knowledge* but they don't normally need technical *skills.*

On occasion I'm called to consult with a firm that's run by an executive who "grew up" on a technical track. He started as a bright engineer, became

FIGURE III-4

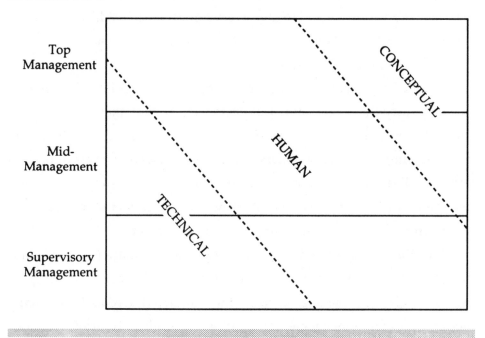

a design team engineer, got promoted to vp engineering, and today, as president, he is floundering because he's developed a very self-limiting personal philosophy: "I never ask anyone to do anything I can't do."

The bad news is that everyone eventually reaches his elastic limit; he simply cannot do it all. He tries to play the valued role of a "hands on" executive and he fails to delegate.

If that's not a bad enough state of affairs, the president has the power to fire anyone in the firm; his judgment could be clouded by his ego, which may be bigger than all outdoors. Now the employees are too intimidated to tell the "big boss" he is flawed. One of the major roles of outside consultants is to tactfully let the senior leaders discover and learn valuable lessons from their own mistakes.

True executives have developed and use their human skills so that they have the ability to ask people to do a myriad of things that they themselves cannot do. When human skills are elevated to an art form, executives can inspire all their employees to willingly accomplish a multitude of tasks better than they did yesterday and to love every minute of it. Just how important are human skills? According to Dr. Katz, all levels of management are dominated by the need for human skills.

I'm told that John D. Rockefeller became a self-made millionaire when he was just thirty-three years old. Ten years later, he was the richest man in America. Ten years later, at age fifty-three, he was the richest man in the world, earning one million dollars per day. That's when he was quoted as saying, "I'll pay more for the ability to deal with people than any other ability under the sun."[6] All my years as a student and practitioner of management put me in perfect agreement with Katz and Rockefeller.

Since this is my book, I'm going to exercise my author's license and dispense a few of my biases. I've found that the difference between good organizations and great ones is clearly the marginal difference between the human skills of the management team. When the leadership, at all levels, can skillfully motivate and effectively lead the work force, the organization invariably succeeds against every measure of merit. It is this basic realization that motivated me to dedicate myself to helping executives and managers sharpen these critical skills.

In order for training or skill development to be effective, you must first determine the skills needed to be successful in a given task. Next, you determine the pertinent skills presently possessed by your employees, and then you establish formal programs to provide the skills needed but not possessed. In other words, you train against the deficit.

The diagnosis of technical skill deficiencies is relatively simple. Old Joe takes a machine apart, cleans it, puts it back together, but there are three pieces left over, and it won't run. It's pretty easy to determine that old Joe does not have the skills needed to put the machine back together properly.

If we are going to be efficient in training Joe, we'll teach him how to put the machine together rather than wasting his time and your money teaching him things he either already knows or doesn't need to know. Think of a fully-trained employee as a full cup. When he or she is not fully trained, the cup is partially full. Effective training first determines the specific deficit, then fills up the cup.

The diagnosis of deficiencies in human skills is much more difficult. I've never seen a supervisor or manager wearing a t-shirt which said, "I'm a rotten supervisor. I turn my people *off* for a living!" You may smile, but the sad part about this is that supervisors who do turn people off are not bad people. They want to succeed in turning their people on, but they simply do not know how.

Quite often, deficiencies in the ability to lead and motivate (turn on) people are covered up with *power*. The mere fact that employees do what they are told *may* mean they have chosen to perform at a minimally acceptable level rather than face the negative consequences the boss can deliver. And power is very seductive. When we see the job getting done, we may fool ourselves into thinking we are providing good leadership. It ain't necessarily so! True leadership exists in the *minds* of the followers. We'll discuss a few ideas on leadership and feedback in Chapter IV.

NOTES ON CHAPTER III

4. Katz, Robert L. "Skills of an Effective Administrator." *Harvard Business Review.* January-February, 1955. 33-42.

5. *Ibid.*, 91.

6. Bergen, Garret L., and William V. Haney. *Organizational Relations and Management Action.* New York. McGraw-Hill Book Company. 1966.

Chapter 4

Feedback— A Leadership Responsibility

As I've mentioned before, one of the greatest causes of performance problems is inadequate feedback. Feedback is one of the all-important consequences which affects a person's willingness to perform effectively. Feedback concepts and skills are so critical to good management that we should examine them in depth.

Millions of dollars and work hours worldwide are devoted to formal performance appraisal/review systems. People at all levels, from janitors to Chairmen of the Board, simply must know—"How am I doing?"

We have found that some managers think that the annual or semiannual formal performance review session takes care of employees' feedback needs; but nothing could be further from the truth. People need feedback on almost a daily basis. In *The One-Minute Manager*, Blanchard and Johnson have printed the following profound statement in bold print on a single page— **"Feedback is the breakfast of champions."**[7] If you want your team to be champions, you must give them balanced feedback every day.

FEEDBACK—THE STERILE CONDUIT

The term "sterile" in this context means objective, candid, unbiased, and most of all, honest. I make very few flat statements when dealing with human behavior, but this is one—"Every healthy system needs feedback." If I had the power to change only one thing in organizational life, I would magically give every manager the willingness and ability to give balanced feedback—both positive and negative. I think feedback is one of the most important aspects of effective leadership and management.

In most work situations, people's self-esteem and sense of accomplishment are related to seeing themselves doing something worthwhile with their work lives. Because most of us prefer the immediate gratification of a short-cycle satisfaction loop, the faster the feedback, the better. With the exception of professional sports, where the score changes the instant a home run is hit or a touchdown scored, most jobs have longer-term feedback systems—monthly or quarterly sales quotas met, products shipped, students educated, buildings completed, and so on. There is a basic variance between the feedback needs of people and the feedback systems inherent in the world of work.

A skillful supervisor/manager is sensitive to this variance and takes action to fill the gap. The supervisor should serve as a real-time conduit of feedback from the long-term goals of the organization as they relate to the specific short-term feedback needs of the employees.

The feedback should keep the employees focused every day on the specific tasks and activities they need to accomplish in order to achieve the long-term goals. Annual performance appraisals are certainly needed, but they're not timely enough. This becomes easier to remember if you imagine everyone perpetually wearing a t-shirt that says, "Make me feel important." Every healthy system needs feedback. If a system is not getting enough feedback to meet its needs, you can bet it isn't healthy.

FEEDBACK GIVEN AT THE TASK LEVEL

People do not do jobs; they do tasks. We train at the task level, lead at the task level, fire at the task level. But, for some unexplained reason, we give feedback at the *job* level. The day you start providing feedback at the task level is the day you become a better manager. Feedback at the *task* level seems to produce a sense of balance, harmony, and equity between the employees and their bosses; it just feels right.

What is the relationship between feedback and leadership? Given that there are over three hundred definitions of leadership, your opinion is as good as mine. But from my vantage point, as a serious student of leadership and management for more years than I like to recall, I see a definite correlation between a person's ability for focusing the efforts of others (leadership) and his or her feedback skills.

Agreed, leadership is the mix of many skills in a countless variety of combinations, but I've found some common threads among most successful leaders: They help people see the vision every day; they help people learn how they are doing; they are skillful at giving feedback. Feedback and positive reinforcement can have a profound impact on motivation and performance.

FEEDBACK—NEVER SAY "PROBLEM"

In giving feedback, the major purpose is to communicate effectively—i.e., to create understanding. The first thing that must occur in the recipient's mind is that he or she must not only hear but actually listen. People generally listen to positive feedback; our egos and self-esteem love to splash and play in rivers of praise.

That same fragile self-esteem has a built-in defense mechanism that helps protect our egos from unwanted negative feedback. As the conversation passes through neutral going south toward criticism, the ego almost automatically turns off the listening process, regardless of the fidelity of our hearing.

Therein lies our dilemma: How do we get people to actually listen to constructive though negative feedback? Let me share with you a consultant's trade secret to short-circuit the automatic cut-off switch when giving negative feedback.

You've got to open the recipient's mind and make him or her *want* to listen. You guessed it—you give him or her *good* news first. Credible, positive feedback works wonders in getting and holding people's attention, because *everyone* needs it, values it, and no one gets nearly enough of it in the world of work.

Notice I said "credible, positive feedback." This requires you to do your homework and to pay attention. When I'm conducting the assessment phase of a consulting engagement, I give equal time to finding things that are working well—systems that perform the way they're supposed to, people who don't stop at the last period in their job description, and so on. If you want to find good news, every organization has plenty; look for it and take good notes. However, since all of us are flawed, and since organizations are made up of groups of flawed people, it's not difficult to find the bad news. When I meet with the responsible manager after studying his or her operation, I start by telling him or her the positive things I've noticed. If you get one level below the glaringly obvious, you'll develop instant credibility as an observant person. So far, they are listening; you are communicating.

Once I have the listener's attention, I need to delicately move from positive facts and opinions to reporting unemotional observations of areas I view as problems. I call that "shining light in dark corners." Let's assume that the organization has a snarl of a backlog in the shipping department. You could say something like, "I was in the shipping department yesterday and noticed some boxes in the far left labeled June 1987; I wondered why they were there."

Let's carefully analyze the wording. The manager's clearly got a backlog problem, but if I describe it as a "problem" he or she may either stop listening or turn hostile because the term "problem" itself is negative, judgmental, and accusatory. What one must do is describe the situation or condition in totally neutral and non-judgmental terms. As the listener begins to visualize the picture I'm painting, he or she mentally compares that picture with what he or she *thinks* is there or *wants* to be there. The client sees the difference

54

between those two pictures as a "problem." They will often say, "It sounds like we have a backlog problem in shipping." The minute managers use the word *problem* of their own free will, they own it. Never say the word "problem" first; let the client do that.

A fellow consultant and I went to lunch recently. He was frustrated because his business was faltering. He holds a doctorate in organization behavior and has many years' experience as a college professor.

After a few minutes of verbally dancing around the deeper issues, he finally blurted out: "I am an expert in solving organizational problems; I can diagnose a problem in a very short time, but I can't seem to get the client to see it. What really bugs me is that I'm a hell of a lot smarter than you are, but you stay busy while my consulting practice is sputtering."

Over the second cup of coffee we discussed the fact that consultants have no power—they have only influence. Diagnosing the problem is a relatively easy first step. The hard part is getting the client (the person with power) to buy in willingly— i.e., to take action and accept personal responsibility for solving the problem. With the responsibility and accountability also goes the credit. My friend now understands that clients not only want to solve their own problems, but they also want to maintain their dignity in the process.

FEEDBACK AND STROKING

When we study transactional analysis, we refer to feedback as "strokes." Positive strokes we call "warm fuzzies" because they make us feel good about the situation and ourselves. Our bag of positive strokes includes praise, recognition, affirmation, listening, and a whole raft of behaviors that are perceived positively by others.

Negative strokes ("cold pricklies") are basically the opposite of warm fuzzies. We see behaviors such as criticism, rebukes, rebuffs, plus all manner of tactless acts as negative strokes.

A plastic stroke is generally positive but so insincere that it calls into question the speaker's credibility. Broad-brush, glittering compliments that describe us as faster than a speeding bullet and able to leap tall buildings in a single bound don't wash well in the business world.

Psychologists tell us that all people have an absolute need for strokes; it's been found that negative strokes are better than no strokes. People will often do things to get attention, even if it results in being scolded. My wife, Liz, is a third-grade school teacher. One September, when her class reported for their first day, she met Toby. Toby was a typical third grader, but my wife seemed to devote a disproportionate amount of her time to Toby.

"Yes, Toby, you may go to the rest room."

"Yes, Toby, you may sharpen your pencil."

"Toby, don't bother Jill."

"Toby, did you just break your pencil?"

"Toby, son, you just went to the bathroom ten minutes ago!"

By 1:00 p.m. Liz had had all of Toby's antics she could stand. By 2:00 p.m., Toby met the principal. Toby had been a discipline problem. His school work and relationships with his classmates were poor and trending down.

A few days later, it was raining; Toby arrived at school a bit early, wearing his little yellow raincoat. Liz is a very nurturing person, so she helped Toby take off his wet raincoat. In the process, she gave him a little hug, saying, "Toby, I hope you don't catch a cold."

Will wonders never cease? All day Toby was a model student. He sat at his desk, stayed on task, completed his assignments, and was pleasant to be around. Toby had a great day!

As the story unfolded, Liz learned that Toby was the fifth of five kids; both parents worked. Everyone was so busy making a living, they didn't have time to make a life.

The only attention Toby got at home was—"Take out the garbage—feed the cat—go to your room." He never got any quality "air-time" with his parents and siblings. Nobody ever asked, "Toby, how are things at school?" He came to school with a deficit of strokes. He had to catch up, and negative strokes are better than no strokes.

For the rest of the year, Toby came to school early, rain or shine, marched religiously up to Mrs. Land's desk for his daily hug. Those simple but important strokes squared the daily deficit. They allowed him to approach his work as a whole person—valued, wanted, loved. Toby had the best year of his academic career. His grades improved and so did his behavior. In fact, he became quite proud of their ritual. "Yep, I get a hug from Mrs. Land every day!" If you feel the inclination to dismiss Toby's story as just kids' stuff—here's an example of a kid in his mid-forties.

At the conclusion of the 1984 Los Angeles Olympics, the young athletes were beginning to fly back to their respective countries for heroes' welcomes. The nation was shocked but relieved to learn that an alert Los Angeles police officer found a bomb which had been hidden in the wheel-well of a jet liner loaded with Olympic athletes. The officer became an instant hero—his name and face appeared in news reports worldwide.

It was learned the next day that *he* had planted the bomb himself. At the press conference which followed, a very embarrassed Police Chief said, "I guess we had a police officer who was not getting enough recognition to meet his needs."

What do Toby, the L.A. police officer, and all of us have in common? Everything—when it comes to our need for strokes. Feedback as a consequence is nothing more or less than effective communication.

FEEDBACK—THE SAINTS AND THE SINNERS

There are scores of definitions for the term "communications." Dr. Donald L. Kirkpatrick's definition in his excellent book *No Nonsense Communications* gets my vote—"Communications means creating understanding."[8]

For the most part, every organizational communication contains two elements. First, there's the "what." The "what" is the main purpose of the communication; it tells us what to do or not to do. Second, the "why" is the reason or logical justification for the "what." The "why" makes the "what" make sense.

As a consultant, I've found that a great majority of organizational problems can be traced back to some failure to communicate—or to create understanding. See if this example is borne out in your experience. The scene is a conference room. A dozen managers, chaired by the CEO, are assembled to solve a problem. The various alternatives are discussed and, finally, one choice appears to be the best course of action. The decision (the what) is ground out of the rationale (the why). The group has been a part of the decision-making process so they jointly see both the "what" and the "why." They understand.

Truism—when the "what" and "why" are attached, the listener will usually understand. Or to say it another way, we have communicated since we have created understanding. So far, so good.

The decision is promulgated and sent to the next level of management. The rub comes when people begin to act like humans. The humans at the second level of management receive the "what and why"—they also understand. But, as they face their obligation to communicate to the subordinate, their egos get in the way. They think, "I understand this decision. But I'm busy and don't have time to share the full story with my staff." So they make a rational decision—"My people need to know the decision (what) but they don't really need to know the background (a portion of the why)." So, they shave off a portion of the "why" and communicate what's left.

The next level has a few gaps in the communication because the background was omitted. The people at that level assess the information needs of their subordinates and decide that their "underlings" don't really need to know the economic impact (a little more of the why is shaved off). The process continues to eat away at the communication as bits and pieces of the "why" are sprinkled down the chain of command. Soon the "what" is standing naked. There's no "why" attached! Now the receiver hears but does not understand.

We have an innate desire to understand; uncertainty and confusion cause stress. The recipient responds to these natural instincts with "Why are we doing this?"

When a supervisor hears that question, particularly when he doesn't know "why" himself, he takes it as defiance or a threat to his authority. The supervisor often responds to questions of "why" with a bluntly stated "Who": "Because the General Manager said so."

The effect of that reply is, "You don't need to know why—only what and who!" Before you had a *curious* employee who didn't understand; now you've got a *hostile* employee who still doesn't understand. That isn't progress and it isn't fun for anyone.

At one time, in an effort to improve communications between me and the one thousand five hundred people in my organization, I played an interesting game with my staff. When my fifteen direct reports and I would pound out a decision at staff meeting, the "what" and "why" were always well understood. My staff may not all have agreed or liked the decision, but they all understood.

Before adjourning the meeting I would usually ask, "Are there any final questions about the 'what and why' of this decision?" If there were, we would clarify them.

Then I would say, "Because it is so important for our people to understand this decision, we are going to play a game called 'Saints and Sinners.' In three days, when I visit the various sections of our organization, I'm going to ask the most junior employees if they can explain both the 'what' and 'why' of this decision. In a word, I'm going to open the valve and see what falls out. If the 'what' and 'why' fall out attached, that's a point for the Saints because everyone in the chain has met the obligation to share the 'what' and 'why'— to create understanding, that is, to communicate. I'm going to reinforce everyone in that channel.

"However, if the 'what' and the 'why' do *not* fall out attached or the 'why' that falls out is so misshapen by half-truths that it makes no sense, then that is a point for the Sinners. I'll start swimming upstream until I find the persons who failed to communicate both the 'what' and 'why' and make them come to my office and explain the 'why' to me."

The amusing part of this story is that I never actually did it, but everyone on my staff thought I was going to do so. Some of my staff told me later they always had two columns in their notebooks—"What" and "Why." I'll let you guess how well my one thousand five hundred employees were informed. Feedback is an essential element of team building.

LEADERS GIVE FEEDBACK

"It's not who leaders are—it's what they do. Leaders are leaders because they do things to help make the dream a reality." —Steve Brown, The Fortune Group International

One thing I've noticed about most successful leaders is that they give high-impact feedback. Most leaders have a vision; they see the organization as it could be, not only as it is today. If the vision is to guide and motivate people, they must be able to see it. The role of a leader is to let people know how their present performance relates to the vision—that's called feedback.

When I see the Readiness x Willingness x Ability = Performance formula for success, I see feedback as the drawstring that ties all the elements together. One of the most important responsibilities of leadership is to provide feedback to subordinates. As we know, people do not do jobs—they do tasks. Therefore, feedback must be given at the task level.

Figure IV-1 helps me in giving feedback. Think of the job as the forest; the tasks are the trees and the various dimensions of the task, branches on the trees.

Every task has a qualitative dimension (it should be done correctly), a quantitative dimension (someone is always counting output), a timeliness dimension (early, on-time, or late), and a cost-effective dimension (one should not use twenty sheets of letterhead to prepare one letter). The

FIGURE IV-1

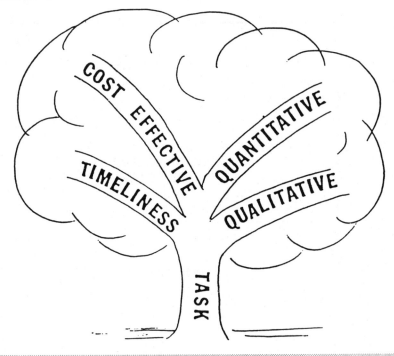

dimensions are actually the standards or expectations associated with each task. For feedback to be effective and of high impact on the subordinate, it should be related to the standards, expressed or implied, of these positive dimensions.

Let's assume I say to my administrative assistant, "Pam, will you please type this letter for me? I need it for my 10:00 meeting." I've asked her to accomplish one of the tasks which make up her job. There's a qualitative dimension (it should be correct), a quantitative dimension (I want *one* letter and one to file), a timeliness dimension (I need it by 10:00), and a cost effective dimension (don't waste our expensive letterhead in the process).

In **Figure IV-2**, the minimally acceptable level of performance (A) for the qualitative dimension is—no typo's, proper format, and neatness. When we look at the quantitative dimension, (A) becomes 2 letters, one to mail and one for the file. The timeliness standard (A) is 10:00. Ten-thirty would represent

FIGURE IV-2

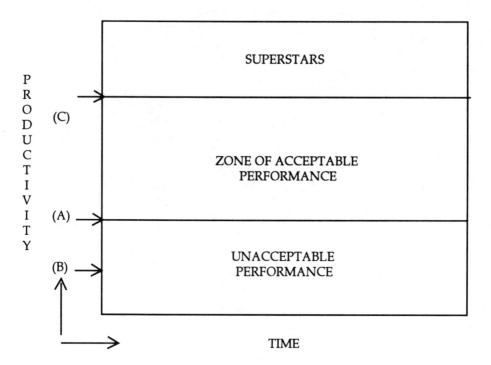

(A) represents the minimally acceptable level of performance for each dimension within each task of the job

a point below the minimally acceptable level (B). However, 8:30 is well above the standard, so I could rightfully see it at point C on the chart. When we view the standard of cost effectiveness, (A) equals one piece of letterhead; using three would be at point (B) on the chart—wasteful.

Let's now assume Pam placed a perfect letter on my desk at 8:30 that morning. If I value opportunities to provide positive reinforcement to Pam, I have an opportunity to praise her for meeting three of the task dimensions, but I'll get the greater impact by singling out the dimension she exceeded—timeliness.

Dr. Dick Leatherman, President of International Training Consultants,

Richmond, Virginia, has developed and marketed some of the finest training materials I've seen. He offers the following first five steps to provide high impact feedback. I've added steps six and seven.

POSITIVE FEEDBACK:

1. Describe the positive situation/incident/behavior in detail. It is best to have first hand knowledge, and then to use first person pronouns: I, me, my.
2. Tell the employee exactly why you value the action taken, i.e., saves time/money, improves quality, etc.
3. Express your personal appreciation for the action.
4. Tell the employee you have confidence in his/her ability to do similar good work in the future.
5. Thank him/her again, shake hands, or pat him/her on the back.
6. You may want to combine the doer and the deed—"That was an excellent piece of work; you're making a fine contribution to the company."
7. Positive feedback may be given in public or private; but public positive feedback is preferred.

I would say, "Pam, thanks for completing this letter early. You gave me an opportunity to fine tune it before the meeting. I appreciate your extra effort on this; if I ever need something done quickly, I know you're there to help. Thanks a lot."

The general output of such behavior on my part almost invariably produces the following response in Pam:

1) She feels her contribution to the mission is genuinely appreciated by her boss.
2) She is more inclined to do the same thing under similar conditions in the future.

3) She also knows that had she made a typographical error, I would have returned it to her to be corrected, which would have robbed her of the full impact of the positive reinforcement. I've found that most people will take that extra moment to check for typo's when they know that positive reinforcement will be forthcoming for good work.

Just as beautiful forests are actually hundreds of healthy trees, good job performance is the result of a multitude of tasks being performed well—above the minimally acceptable level of performance. Everyone appreciates the beauty of a forest; similarly, effective managers take pride in the high performance of their employees.

It's management folklore that "You get what you reinforce." That point was driven home to me powerfully during one of my visits to an off-shore oil production platform. The crew was experiencing some production problems, and I was asked to see if I could determine the cause and help them "get well."

The Superintendent was in his mid-fifties and had grown up in the oil patch. He was tough by any measure of merit and took pride in running his crew with an iron hand. He sincerely felt the company paid his people to do a good job, and it was his charter to be sure the company got its money's worth. He said, "I've got pretty good men, but they will goof off if I let them."

He had developed a behavior pattern of strongly confronting screw-ups (deviations). When I asked if he ever confronted good work (praise) he said, "If I became too wimpy, they would lose respect for me and I'd lose control. I'm not out here to win a popularity contest; I'm out here to get the oil out of the Gulf."

The basic reason his crew was experiencing performance problems was that they were all doing only minimum work. The superintendent did not understand the following basic truism about people.

If you punish people severely enough for deviations, you may change their behavior, but only to the extent that they will stop doing bad things. They will do enough work to avoid the unwanted consequences—punishment. However, this process does not ensure that they will do *good* things. The opposite of bad things is not good—the absence of bad things equals minimally acceptable performance—that is, mediocrity, the precursor to bankruptcy.

After we chatted with the superintendent over coffee, he had a profound revelation. "I guess we don't get the oil out of the Gulf by all my men *not* doing stupid things, we get the oil out by their *doing* smart things." He took notes on Dick Leatherman's five steps to positive feedback. On last report, they are doing a much better job of getting the oil out of the Gulf.

Providing feedback to senior management is one of the obligations of management consultants. In the mid-1970s, I was the director of management consultation for the United States Air Force. Our directorate was formed by Air Force Chief of Staff General David C. Jones, to offer the same kind of consulting services to senior Air Force officials as the consulting industry provides for business and industry leaders.

Rest assured that the military had little experience in working with leadership and management consultants in the 1970s. In fact, some senior officers still don't believe management consultants are of value in a military environment.

In February 1977, I led a team of Air Force consultants on a five-week trip to work for several installation commanders in Hawaii and the Far East. All Air Force units in the Pacific Air Command reported to a four-star general headquartered at Hickam Air Force Base in Hawaii.

Since we had a confidential relationship with the installation commanders, normally senior colonels or one-star generals, we did not provide detailed feedback to the four-star generals on the problems we helped resolve for our client organizations. If we had, we would have been no more than another inspection team. Inspectors tend to put people at risk and, therefore, people are very guarded in discussing their problems. In order for us to have a positive impact on our client's organization, we had to develop and maintain a relationship of confidentiality.

One of my responsibilities was to pay a courtesy call on the four-star general at Hickam AFB to explain our role so as to be sure he understood he would not receive a detailed "out-briefing" on the problems we found at each base. I had to ensure that he understood and supported our policy of "no up-channel reporting."

I had a five-minute appointment scheduled for 5:00 p.m. I entered the handsome office to find one of the most impressive officers I've ever seen. He was in his late fifties, with more ribbons on his chest than I thought possible. If the truth were known, I was awestruck. After returning my salute, he invited me to be seated.

I'll never forget his opening comment: "I understand you're leading a team of management consultants to help us achieve our mission better. I have one question, Colonel. What right do *you* have to tell *me* how to be a four-star general?"

That was perhaps one of the toughest questions of my professional career. The answer I came up with dealt squarely with the true value of honest, candid feedback to management.

As best I can recall, I said something like: "Sir, first, let's clear the air on one point. I am not here as a forty-year-old colonel to personally advise you in your role as a general officer. You have, no doubt, forgotten more about leadership and management than I personally know. But I have a team of talented and highly trained consultants who are going to study your organization for the next several weeks. They will interview, observe, and survey thousands of the people who carry out your mission. Our consultants are going to place stethoscopes on the heart of your organization; we will listen to its pulse. Since leadership exists in the minds of the followers, we are going to determine the perceived effectiveness of the overall leadership of your command. I'm here to ensure that our teams provide a sterile conduit of feedback to leaders at every level. With this feedback they should be able to

66

grow, to develop, to become better leaders. So, General, *I'm* not going to tell you how effective you are as a leader, but we are going to provide the vehicle for thousands of your followers to tell you how they feel about your leadership."

I detected a knowing smile as he peered over his reading glasses and said, "By damn, Colonel, I've got to buy that!" I had one of the most fascinating hour-long discussions I've ever had with that outstanding military leader.

STUDENTS ARE HONORED FOR THEIR PERSONAL EFFORTS— LEADERS ARE HONORED THROUGH THE EFFORTS OF OTHERS

I think our colleges and universities fail to stress an absolutely critical point when preparing our graduates and MBA's to assume positions of leadership. The consequence system in our educational institutions is based on honoring the student for his or her individual efforts. The report cards and diploma only have one name on them.

The rub comes when the graduate enters the world of leadership and management where his or her true success is attributable to the efforts of others. I've seen young managers meet their needs for personal recognition by taking credit for the work of their subordinates. Not only is this tacky and professionally dishonest, it sounds the death knell for your employees' willing cooperation for the next millennium.

I've learned that there is almost no limit to what an organization can do when the manager shoulders the blame but shares the credit. For some inexplicable reason, many managers get that simple phrase reversed; they shoulder the credit and share the blame.

LEADERSHIP VS. POWER

It's important for everyone in a leadership position to understand the precarious balance between position power and leadership. This point was best brought home to me during my Air Force career.

Second Lieutenant Bill Harrell graduated from an Eastern college with a degree in mechanical engineering and received his commission through the Air Force ROTC program. After completing Aircraft Maintenance Officer's School, he reported to an Air Force Base in Texas as a Flight Line Maintenance Officer. This twenty-two-year-old was assigned a small, private office and thirty enlisted personnel. His senior subordinate was a master sergeant with over twenty-five years' experience in aircraft maintenance and a chest full of ribbons which reflected his skill and professionalism.

The sergeant had experience, judgment, and the earned respect of the troops. About all the lieutenant had was position power—more power than he had ever had before. If someone failed to do what he directed, the Uniformed Code of Military Justice gave him the power to put them in prison.

He soon learned he could yell from his office, "Hey, Sarge, get in here!" and the sergeant came—every time. The lieutenant had almost total control of a man who was older than his father! The sergeant's not responding to the lieutenant was not a viable option; the lieutenant had more position power than the sergeant.

The lieutenant had learned how to use position power to control the sergeant's *behavior;* but what do you think was happening to the sergeant's *attitude*? It was going south at the speed of light.

Since one of my jobs as a colonel was to raise our second lieutenants, it was time for the lieutenant and the colonel to go to lunch. Over our second cup of coffee, somehow the conversation got around to leadership, position power, attitudes, and behavior. When I'd laid the proper conceptual background and the lieutenant understood how seductive position power could be, I said, "Bill, if you have to use the authority inherent in that gold bar on your shoulder to get your sergeant to respond, then you ought not to be wearing it. The art of officership and leadership is to get that sergeant to give his all to the mission even if you have no position power at all."

We talked about the great opportunity Bill had to learn about aircraft maintenance from a consummate expert—his sergeant. We talked about delegation, teamwork, and praise.

Over the next few weeks, I'd rarely see the lieutenant without the sergeant; they became an unbeatable team built upon mutual respect. Many years later, when Bill Harrell was a major and had been decorated for exceptional performance as a chief of maintenance, I ran into his old sergeant and mentor.

"Sarge, did you hear about Major Harrell's being presented a medal last month?"

"Yes, Sir, I did. He called me long distance. You know something, Colonel, I'm proud of Major Harrell; I helped raise him."

"You sure did, Sergeant, you sure did."

FEEDBACK—LARGE MOSAIC

How do I motivate my employees? I'm asked that question repeatedly by men and women from all walks of managerial life. One way to create a climate for self-motivation is to ensure that everyone knows that his or her job and specific contributions are important.

I view an organization like a mosaic. We often stand in awe of a large mosaic — an impressive picture made up of hundreds of small pieces of glass. If I were to remove one tiny piece of glass and place it in someone's hand and ask, "What do you have in your hand?" they would undoubtedly reply, "A piece of broken glass." But if I take them to the mosaic and let them watch me return the glass to its rightful place in the mosaic, then instantly that piece of broken glass becomes important—it gains significance from its position in the mosaic—it now has value.

There is a close parallel between a mosaic and an organization. Every person in an organization is as important as every piece of glass in a mosaic. When feedback is practiced as an art form, all employees are shown how they contribute to the larger organizational goals—how they fit into the impressive mosaic. I've consistently found in healthy organizations that everyone sees him or herself in an important position.

TIME FOR SOME POSITIVE REINFORCEMENT

I was called to a company recently and found a situation where commitment and morale were low. I started looking for a way to say "You're important, you're good for this organization" to the employees. Remember, if you say it in a big way to one person, word gets around. This is the way we handled it.

I asked a supervisor if the company had an outstanding employee program, and he said, "Sure."

"Who's your best employee?" was my next question.

"Mary," he replied.

"Have you recommended Mary for the outstanding employee award?" I asked.

"Well, no. I haven't nominated Mary because she probably wouldn't get it anyway," the guy said.

Talking to this supervisor was like pulling teeth. He didn't seem too excited that the out-of-town consultant had chosen his department to poke around in. And I wasn't sure whether I should be looking for a motivation problem with the workers or with the supervisor.

If Mary is, in fact, the supervisor's best employee, the most credible in the department, the supervisor has an obligation to sit down with the forms, regulations, and guidelines and prepare his input to the board nominating Mary. To do that, he has to investigate her job performance and growth, her contribution, and the dollar impact of her work on the company. In addition, to make her a viable competitor as an outstanding member of the organization, the supervisor should also become aware of Mary's contributions outside the workplace. Perhaps she is a member of a civic organization, works in her community, or with the youth at her church. He has to see Mary as more than an employee doing a job. The bottom line is, if any employee represents or exceeds the standards of the company, he or she should be identified and recognized.

70

The supervisor got the idea.

He drafted a report nominating Mary for Outstanding Employee honors. He even called Mary and asked her to validate some of his information. That action let her know that her name was being submitted. The supervisor sent his report to the board for consideration.

A few weeks later, Mary got a letter from the board saying: "Dear Mary, we appreciate your fine work; however, you were not selected, ..."

Did Mary win or lose?

She won.

The important relationship is not between Mary and the board, but between Mary and her supervisor; that is the one that matters. When he identified her by nominating her for the best employee, he was saying to other people in the department who observe her, as well as to Mary, "This is what we are looking for; this is the standard we want to honor."

Mary was motivated to do an even better job next year, and the people who watched her work knew what the reference points were by the actions of management. The overall goal was to clone Mary among her co-workers.

The mere fact that Mary did not receive the company-wide award is not important. The nomination made a statement to the department. It said, "Our supervisor cares about us."

This is the motivation business. Remember this—*People do not poke holes in boats they are in.* Management's objective is to get subordinates in the boat and make them see themselves as part of the organization—to see themselves in the mosaic. When they are not in the boat, they poke holes—get to work late, do the absolute minimum, and leave precisely on time.

If the people in your organization are not in the boat, they'll be "clock eyed." They'll be waiting impatiently for the moment they don't have to work any more—quitting time. You'll find them very conversant on what is *not* their job and where their obligations to the company *end.*

When they are in the boat, they get possessive. It's *our* plant, *our* equipment, *our* mission. It is not how management sees them, but how they see themselves. Getting in the boat means that they will paddle and bail, and that's working long hours and being creative and going far beyond the last period in the job description.

AN EFFECTIVE LEADER PERSONIFIES THE MISSION

An organization needs both a mission and goals. Its mission is its overall purpose, the condition it is supposed to sustain. Its goals are the supporting elements of the mission. The mission is the sign out front; the goals are the posts that hold the sign up. It's the actual goals that we accomplish to achieve the mission.

Job and mission are not the same. Your job is the array of tasks you are expected to perform. Your mission involves a moral compulsion to perform; it's your calling.

Before people will get in the boat—whether it be a meeting to plan a church budget, a research group looking for a cure for cancer, or an industry building heavy machinery—they have to understand and buy into that organization's mission. And before they will buy in, they have to be able to answer the following questions to their own satisfaction:

1. Why are we here?
2. What's the purpose of this organization?
3. What are our long-range goals?
4. What are our immediate objectives?

The answers to those questions will clarify the organization's mission in their minds.

It's the responsibility of managers and leaders to communicate an organization's mission so that subordinates want to buy in, so that they do not have a near-sighted vision of purpose. Individuals can get so wrapped up in doing their job that they lose sight of the reason behind it. They fail to identify with the mission. And when they lose sight of the mission, they become "assembly line workers" instead of a team building a fine automobile.

An effective manager will continually translate organizational mission to a personal level for subordinates. When you, as a leader, identify with a mission strongly and clearly, the people around you will see the mission through you.

Consider an organization with a sign out front that says "XYZ Company." The employees don't identify with that company; they see the president or the person who becomes the moral leader—the focus of leadership. If they respect the leader, they will be proud to be a member of the company. And if they identify positively with the company, they will identify with the mission and will not begrudge their personal efforts to achieve it.

You may find a person who says, "I don't have any role in the mission. I just work in the mail room." The mail room is very important in achieving the overall administrative mission, so if you can get that individual to say, "I work in support of the administration of this company," they have bought into a higher mission.

But if the person in primary leadership focus has not connected with his or her people, they will not feel comfortable about their leadership and, in turn, won't support the mission. Consequently, they will begrudge the time and effort they spend to accomplish that mission.

A mission does not have to be company-wide. Your mission can be located within the shipping department or an assembly room. But wherever you find your personal mission, it must be crystal clear.

The key is that your efforts should be focused totally on the mission of your organization. The mission has to "burn in your belly." Everything you do should be designed to accomplish or enhance the mission. If something doesn't achieve the mission, don't do it, but if it is directed toward achieving your primary mission, throw yourself into it with wild abandon.

As the members of an organization begin to coalesce around the mission, they will start to present ideas, become enthusiastic, and get involved. They will begin to perceive the mission—which is greater than their individual jobs or goals. Keep in mind that a mission at the organizational or corporate level is generally more satisfying and gratifying to identify with personally.

All managers must be aware of a subtle relationship involved in translating an organization's mission. When a person gives to a mission, the mission doesn't give back; so in effect, the giver's needs aren't being met unless he or she can personally see his or her long-term impact on the mission. As a manager, if you are the focus of the mission, then you have to do your dead-level best to return to your subordinates—in the short run, through effective interpersonal skills—the organization's appreciation for their contribution to the mission.

If a person makes a contribution to a mission, you must listen, appraise, and reflect the credit for the contribution. Give reinforcement immediately, but keep it on a mission level. People need to know almost on a heartbeat-by-heartbeat basis that they are on target, that they are making a contribution, and that it is valued by management.

Say, "Your effort has allowed us to accomplish this mission" quicker or better or cheaper. Don't say, "You have made my job a lot easier." It isn't your mission, although you personify it. Refer to the mission at all times as "our mission" or "the mission." You simply become the conduit for subordinates' energy and loyalty that flows through you to the mission. In turn, you serve as a process interactor, allowing the mission to speak to your employees through your interpersonal skills in terms of reinforcing them for their contribution. If a mission is completed, they get the credit; if it fails, you take the blame. It's never, "my department." It's always "we" or "us" or "our." The credit always goes to the people who are at the bottom doing the job, making things happen.

Living in Alabama, I am a long-time fan of the famous football coach, Paul "Bear" Bryant. In the film "Nothin' But A Winner," Coach Bryant assumes complete responsibility for every aspect of a student/athlete's life except for one—"I'm responsible for everything but their courtin'. I can't handle that. But if he didn't play well on Saturday, maybe I should not have recruited him or I didn't have him ready to play mentally." He gives them the credit for winning but assumes total and complete responsibility for a loss. It takes broad shoulders to share the credit and accept the blame; Coach Bryant had very broad shoulders.

LEADERSHIP ABILITY IS A VARIABLE, NOT A CONSTANT

For years we've heard about "born leaders" and "natural leaders." I want to add my biases to the already brimming body of biases about the subject of natural leadership.

There is no such thing as a born leader any more than there are born brain surgeons. I accept that leadership is primarily the understanding and application of a variety of discrete skills. One important input skill to leadership is the ability to communicate values and ideas effectively.

Some people seem to be born with more natural talent for certain things than other people. My son has a talent for music, my daughter for math, I for neither. The so-called "natural" leaders have taken their inborn proclivity for a certain skill and through the three-step process of work, work, and more work, have elevated that skill to the highest level of their potential. Anything done well looks easy or natural.

A prime example comes from my home town, Wilmington, North Carolina. I have friends in Wilmington who tell about a skinny youth who played basketball on the city courts all during basketball season. But, strangely, he was also there, often alone, during football and baseball seasons. This young lad practiced his shots year-round, often in inclement weather.

He had some natural ability but he applied the three "D's": diligence, discipline, and dogged determination to raise his talent to an art form. Today, millions of spectators marvel at the "natural ability" of perhaps the most outstanding professional basketball player of our era—Michael Jordan.

When I conduct leadership development workshops, I stress that everyone in the room has the potential to enhance his or her own leadership ability. You improve your leadership ability as you develop any other skill—by understanding the concepts and then practicing the skills—old-fashioned work, work, and more work. Leadership ability is a variable—not a constant.

NOTES ON CHAPTER IV

7.   Blanchard, Kenneth, and Spencer Johnson. *The One-Minute Manager*. New York. Berkley Books. 1983.

8.   Kirkpatrick, Donald L. *No Nonsense Communications*. Elm Grove, Wisconsin. K & M Publishers. 1983.

Chapter 5

R x W x A = P for Performance: The Formula for Success

As we reflect on the ideas expressed in this book, we find an immutable truth. Success in any organizational setting involves interaction of these three important variables—R for readiness (resources), W for willingness (consequences in balance), and A for ability (knowing how and knowing you know how).

The P in the formula can be profit, productivity, or any other valued output of the system, regardless of how large or small. Take particular note that the three main variables interact in a multiplicative, not an additive, manner.

If we had ten units of readiness, ten units of willingness, and ten units of ability, we could expect one-thousand units of output. However, if we had twenty units of readiness, twenty units of willingness, but decided we would postpone or cancel the training, A (ability) drops to zero; the result is not four hundred but zero. The rules of math dictate that anything multiplied by zero nets zero.

The major message for managers is that we should direct our energies and attention to ensuring we keep the three balls (labeled R, W and A) as high as possible in our organizations. When you, as a manager, create an environment where the company, the employees, and you all win simultaneously and continuously, it's really fun to come to work.

It's exciting to lead and motivate people. My mission in this book has been to help you accomplish your mission in your organization. I want to give you some "user friendly" tools that you can take into the workplace, and use.

Working with people is far more complicated than working with machines and computers. A solution that worked today in engineering will also work tomorrow, but a solution that worked today in the human system may or may not work tomorrow. The human factor has so many dynamic variables that you simply can't use a cookie-cutter approach; the concept R x W x A = P seems however, to surface as a winner repeatedly.

When you work with equipment, you have to be aware of the mean failure curve. When you put a load on a piece of machinery and stress it, it will eventually wear out or fail. Every time you use a piece of machinery, you move it closer to failure; you leave it weaker than when you picked it up.

Effective managers use their skills to build people. In a word, every time a manager interacts with an employee (human system), the manager should leave the employee stronger. Your employees should go home every day a little smarter, more dedicated and confident, more professionally developed because they were in your sphere of influence. This feeling of growth and development is like an aphrodisiac for both the managers and their employees—it turns everyone on to the mission.

LEVELS OF CHANGE

The major reason you read this book was to improve your behavior—to make you better than you were yesterday. Before any significant change can occur, there are three steps that must take place in the proper sequence. Dr. Kurt Lewin contributed the ideas of unfreezing, change, and refreezing to our field.[9] The first step is termed "unfreezing." Unfreezing is a process whereby you must personally devalue what you are presently doing. Today, you have your own way to deal with people, your way to run meetings, your way to provide feedback, your way you task employees or provide criticism. The reason you do things the way you do is because they are habits. They are habits because you value those particular skills and behaviors.

In order to replace those habits or skills with better habits, you must devalue those presently in that habit niche. Unfreezing occurs only when you decide that the particular skill you are now using no longer holds high value for you. Unfreezing actually takes place at gut level. You have to say to yourself, "Self, there is a better way. I can be better when it comes to this particular management skill."

As a consultant, I may devalue the method a client is now using, and I counsel the client to improve the way he or she is handling a particular management decision or issue. However, if my clients do not devalue what they're doing, I get an argument. I hear "Yes, but..." or "We're unique," or "You don't understand," or "It won't work here," or all of the above. What they're actually saying is, "I value what I'm doing more than I value the change you are suggesting," and consequently, they never change because they never unfreeze. However, when they see the benefits and values of the new skill relative to the present behavior, they will conclude, "There is a better way," and unfreeze.

Let's assume that you're holding a particular skill (management tool) in your hand. The reason you're holding it is because you value it. The only way a new skill can be put in your hand and become internalized as a habit is for you to remove or release the one that's presently there. If I tried to pull a valued tool out of your hand, you would grip it tightly, as we tend to grip emotionally those things that we still value. Unfreezing must take place willingly within the person.

The next step of the process is the "change" itself or the implementing of the new skill—e.g., a new way of understanding organization performance, or a new way of providing praise to an employee. In dealing with people, we generally find that if we can understand the new skill and practice it, then that skill will soon be valued and become ours.

People normally go through what is known as the "fuzzy phase," awkwardness, until they build confidence through practice. In our workshops, we practice the skills to the point that when the participants leave, they feel the skill is part of them, and they have the confidence to use that skill in their work setting.

The final step is "refreezing." Refreezing occurs when the new skill becomes a habit and it locks in, becomes internalized. You internalize the new skill because it's now highly valued. The main reason it's valued is that you've used it successfully during the "fuzzy phase." Now that skill is a part of you.

Habits are the chains of the free; they make us what we are. I've seen many managers who are "unconscious competents" at the skills of leading and managing. They can simply walk into an organization and, in a matter of minutes, the people sense their effectiveness because of their skill and ability to communicate and motivate. Their very presence raises the morale and the productivity in the organization. They have this power today because they have practiced good management habits successfully for years; they are unconscious competents.

In closing my seminars, I often ask this question of the group with respect to change: "How many people in this room can ride a bicycle?" Most people raise their hand. The next question, "How many of you rode a bicycle properly the very first time? Just got on the two-wheeler, with no training wheels, and pedaled off down the street?" Not many people raise their hand. I ask in jest, "You mean you fell off the bicycle several times like I did? I recall, as a small child, when I had fallen off my first bicycle for the twentieth time, I had scraped all the bark off my knees and elbows, and I was crying; I was convinced that riding a two-wheeler was impossible! You need at least three wheels. But I climbed back on—I went through the fuzzy phase—since the change from walking to riding a bicycle was a highly valued change. I continued to get back on and one day I didn't fall off. Now all of us ride bicycles as unconscious competents. We do it instinctively because that skill has been refrozen, locked in; it is part of us. In fact, most people do not know how *not* to ride a bicycle; it's almost difficult *not* to ride one properly. Why? Because it's a locked-in change, a refrozen skill."

80

Keep this thought in mind as you use the skills in this book. You'll understand that the skills we discussed are easier to master than riding a bicycle. When they become a part of your habit patterns, they'll have great value to you in becoming an effective leader and manager in any organization.

Every failure I have had in the leadership and management fields can be traced back to my not using the principles well, to my either not understanding the concepts, or my simply not applying them. When I have failed and have gone back to do an autopsy on the failure, I find that I'm responsible—that I got cute and tried to say, "This doesn't apply to me." It's a poor craftsperson who blames the tools. And when you apply the concept R x W x A = P, you will find that it will work every time.

Allow me to lower the curtain on this book with one of the most profound and heart-warming experiences of my life. In this true but unbelievable story are all the elements of R x W x A = P played out in dramatic style. Don't lose the deeper truths in the excitement of the story; the keen observer will see readiness, willingness, and ability in the positive and balanced interaction that produces a championship football team. The players were children, but they performed like true professionals.

As I mentioned earlier, when I returned from Viet Nam in the fall of 1972, I was assigned as an Air Force Tactical Officer at my alma mater, The Citadel, Charleston, South Carolina. My family and I lived in the nearby community of Mount Pleasant.

When school started in September, my eight-year-old son, Steve, who was a good athlete, indicated he wanted to play Pee Wee football. There were six teams in the 8-10 year olds' Pee Wee League—the Raiders, Cowboys, Vikings, Dolphins, etc. Steve was assigned, at random, to the Vikings team.

The next day we learned that in the 1971 season, the Vikings had scored one touchdown all year. They tied that game 6 to 6; they lost all the others. The Vikings were the uncontested "door-mat" of the Pee Wee League.

Trying to make the best out of a bad situation, I remarked philosophically to my wife, Liz, "This is going to be a character-building season for Steve; he's going to learn to lose ten straight games and still be a good sport."

We heard that the Vikings had been assigned a new coach, Billy Davies, who had played some football in college. I thought, "This new coach could certainly do no worse than his predecessor."

Within a few days we settled into the family routine of the fall activities. Liz would pick up Steve from school, take him home to put on his football uniform, then drive him several miles to the practice field. I would stop by the field around 5:00 to watch the last hour and a half of practice. Finally I would take my tired and dirty eight-year-old home for a bath, dinner, homework, and much needed rest.

The first day of practice, the parents were exchanging greetings and trying to find something good to say about this group of great kids who had joined this truly rotten football team. It was common practice to ask a few dads to serve as assistant coaches. Their main role was to provide a little adult supervision and to do basically what the head coach asked. I was invited to assist; I consented with the clear understanding that my football experience was limited to sand-lot teams over twenty-five years before.

Billy Davies was a very knowledgeable football coach and was a pleasure to work with. Shortly after the beginning of the practice sessions, he asked me about my background and experience. I explained I had been used in the Air Force as a trouble shooter. I said, "My main jobs have been to solve problems in Air Force units."

He said, "If you just look out on that practice field, you can see we have lots of problems!"

After practice, Billy and I decided to see if the concepts and principles I had used in troubled organizations would help the Pee Wee Vikings football team. We divided the tasks—Billy would teach them the game of football and I would mold them into a team.

It was clear that the major reason for non-performance was a lack of skill and knowledge, so we set up a highly organized training program to teach

82

the fundamentals of the game. We also were faced with low self-esteem and poor morale. It is a basic truth that people, at all ages, learn more, learn faster, and make fewer mistakes when their self-esteem is high. These kids needed mega-doses of confidence and pride.

After the first week of practice, Coach Davies called the Vikings together for a brief chat. If I live to be one hundred years old I'll never forget his next words: "Fellows, we've been together for about a week and I see some real talent on this team. We've got to work on our fundamentals, but I think we can field a pretty good ball team. In fact, I'm going to predict that the Vikings are going to win the championship in the Pee Wee League *this* year."

That's a tall order for the second smallest team in the league and the worst team the previous year. But as I looked in the eyes of those little boys, I could see they actually *believed* they were going to be the champions.

A few days later I asked Sam David Taylor, an eighty-five-pound defensive tackle, "Son, what position do you play?"

He looked me squarely in the eye and stated confidently, "Sir, I play in the other team's backfield."

A week later I approached the defensive line who was waiting for the huddle to break. "Aren't you guys worried where the next offensive play is going?" The defensive captain yelled the question to his team, "Where's the next play going?" They all shouted in unison, "NOWHERE!" The vaccination of pride and self-esteem was beginning to take.

Let's take a backward glance at the specific steps we took to create such a positive attitude. First, we said that if you are going to *be* champions, you must *act* like champions. Question—how do champions act? Answer—(1) Champions keep at least a "C" average in all subjects. (2) Champions eat properly and get adequate rest. (3) Champions learn the plays and football rules. (4) Champions get to practice on time and keep their equipment in good condition. (5) Champions do what they are asked to do without complaining. (6) Champions work together—as a team.

We established a policy that players could only give positive feedback (praise) to other teammates. If one player criticized another player, the errant player was either benched or made to run extra laps around the field at the end of practice. I assure you both of these actions were considered punishment (negative consequences).

The psychological payoff was that the players bonded together. They actually enjoyed blocking for and helping each other. When mistakes were made, the coaches would ask, "Jimmy, can you tell us what you could have done differently so you could have made that tackle?" This technique forced the players to think through and learn from every mistake.

As the pre-season drills continued, we could see an amazing transformation taking place. This group of kids who included rich and poor, black and white, were becoming a team. They developed respect for each other; the good students began to tutor the weaker students; they all shared the same team values and one common, highly-valued goal—to win the championship this year.

As you know, confidence over-extended is arrogance, so shortly before the first game, we met with our team to discuss the difference between well-founded confidence and shallow arrogance. We agreed that we would not boast of our goal to anyone. Not only would it be in bad taste, but we wanted our first opponent to walk on the field over-confident based on last year's record. We explained that their over-confidence could sap that little extra effort that true winners possess. We wanted our opponents to have that problem—not us.

Well, the Vikings played out the season—they won ten straight games! They scored a total of 219 points that season and their defense gave up a total of nineteen points in ten games—less than two points per game. The Vikings were the uncontested *champions* of the Pee Wee League.

The Mount Pleasant Recreation Department had traditionally selected the top two players on each of the six teams and honored them as All-Stars; thirteen Vikings were designated as County-Wide All-Stars. I was bursting with pride when I learned that my son, Steve, had made the All-Star Team.

84

Remember Sam David Taylor? He led the league with more than one-hundred tackles. Guess where many of them were? Right—in the other team's backfield.

Since the Vikings were so formidable, the coaches and league officials proposed an unprecedented idea. They selected the five best players on the other five teams and formed a twenty-five-man team, coached them for two weeks, and played the Vikings in an exhibition game. They wanted to see if any team could beat the Vikings.

The big event was a cold Saturday morning in November; the stands were packed; the media turned out in force to see this Cinderella team in action. The Vikings won that game 12-0 and only gave up one first-and-ten.

At the frenzied finish, the reporters crowded around the team and Coach Davies. "Coach, how did you accomplish this near-miracle of taking the Vikings from the worst to the best virtually overnight? What is your secret to coaching football?"

"Ladies and gentlemen," he replied, "when we first met with these kids, they had the equipment, they were motivated to play, but what they lacked was the ability. The basic skills were *not* in place. All we did was to treat them as champions, which maintained their self-esteem, then taught them the fundamentals of football until they became instinctive. After the drills and practices, they knew how to block and tackle *perfectly;* these kids became 'unconscious competents.'"

The lesson we can learn from the Pee Wee Vikings is profound. First, make an honest assessment of the reasons for non-performance. The Vikings at the beginning of the season had everything but skills and confidence. Second, train against the deficit. We gave the Vikings the skills they needed to be successful but did not possess. Third, project high expectations to sustain positive motivation and willingness. That's how we, and you, put points on the scoreboard or profits in the bank.

The success Billy Davies and I had with those kids had nothing to do with creativity; the things we did were as old as Methuselah. The operative words in the last sentence are "we did." Many coaches and managers *know* the fundamentals; lots of people can *talk* a good game. But in sports and business, there's little payoff for talking; there's not much value in dormant potential or unused skills. Teams and organizations win only when coaches and managers *actually apply* those proven leadership and management skills properly. What do Coach Davies and every other winner in the world have in common? They put the fundamentals into practice.

At the beginning of this book, I promised to share with you a few ideas and skills that can help you manage to get the job done, and win in the game of managing people. Here you have it: **R x W x A = P**—a proven formula to help you **lead your organization to top performance—and have fun doing it.** I have never met a winner who wasn't having fun.

NOTES ON CHAPTER V

9.   Lewin, Kurt. "Frontiers In Group Dynamics: Concept, Method, and Reality in Social Science; Social Equilibria and Social Change." *Human Relations*, I, No. 1 (June 1974). 5-41.

Consulting/ Training Tips

One of management's first responsibilities is to put the skills in place. High-quality training is expensive; as always, you get what you pay for. No one disagrees that training is essential. The key question is, How do you train effectively and efficiently?

It's been my experience that most adults do not relish being directed to attend training programs. Perhaps this reluctance is due to our memories of high school or college days when some teachers tended to make us feel somewhat inadequate in their subject, particularly when compared to them. Since we all bring our egos and self-esteem to work, any situation which seems to threaten one or both of these critical facets of our personalities are usually approached unenthusiastically, at best. But the more enthusiasm we bring to the classroom, the more we learn. Therein lies one of the basic dilemmas of adult educators.

Over the years, I've learned a few tips that help take the "ouch" out of seminars/workshops and which help improve the chances for truly meaningful learning to take place.

The student should have some input on what's being taught. This not only helps clarify the true deficit, but subtly plants those critical seeds of participation, acceptance, and ownership. The training department, or management, may actually know the precise needs of the student, but there's no substitute for the student's hearing him or herself say in an interview, "...If I were going to design a training program to make me more effective, I'd want to learn more about..." The first step in learning is the personal

87

realization that you need to learn, that you have deficits in your knowledge and skills. Dr. Kurt Lewin terms this process *"unfreezing"*; we discussed this concept in Chapter V. I'm reminded of a wise old sage who mused, "Half of being smart is knowing what you're dumb at."

The second precept for success is that the training must be experiential. This means the students must become actively involved in role-plays, games, and projects so that they can practice the learned skill and gain confidence. Most adults are so image-conscious and inhibited that they won't try a new skill the very first time back on the job with subordinates or co-workers, for fear of doing it poorly. That's exactly why in our seminars we stress that we are fortunate to be in a "Rubber Room." You are safe to try the new skill, make those inevitable little goofs, but no one gets hurt. We build a safety net of caring within the seminar to help get everyone through the "fuzzy phase." It's important for the students to know the skill, but it's crucial to let them *know* they *know*. That's why we make it experiential and let them practice.

I recall when I went through parachute training as a forty-four-year-old Air Force Colonel. After what felt like endless repetitions of the parachute landing falls in a soft sand box from a four-foot platform, one of our class members groaned, "I guess practice makes perfect." "Wrong," barked our outstanding instructor with over three thousand parachute jumps. "Practice only makes *permanent*. Perfect practice makes perfect!"

That old soldier knew his business. He insisted that we set our standards high, strive for perfection, and then practice perfection. When you practice new skills in the training sessions, don't expect perfection at first, but don't be satisfied until the students are comfortable executing them properly.

I'm confident that untold new skills have never been used in the work place because normally inhibited students have not had the confidence to risk being embarrassed by "looking awkward" in front of their subordinates. Practice sessions are absolutely essential if you want the new skills to be applied back on the job.

The final precept in effective training is that there should be some positive rapport between the students and the teachers. Most outside trainers and consultants begin their relationship in a seminar with a headwind of doubt and skepticism from the participants. You can see strong non-verbal messages from the students that say "What can this person tell me about the management problems in my industry?"

However, if the trainer has met in advance with some or all of the participants, on their turf, there is a completely different atmosphere in the room. The usual awkward introductions are replaced with, "Good morning, Joe, it's good to see you again."

As a trainer, it helps to maintain your humility when you realize that everyone is superior to you in some way. The key is finding that special knowledge niche each person fills in life, then letting him or her take pride in that uniqueness.

As the training sessions begin, it's absolutely critical to create the optimum learning relationship between the participants and the teacher, as well as among the students themselves. The following technique has served me well for many years.

I write the following on a flip chart:

INTRODUCTIONS
(BUDDY SYSTEM)

- NAME
- ORGANIZATION/POSITION
- HOW MANY YEARS HAVE YOU BEEN IN MANAGEMENT?
- HOW MANY PEOPLE REPORT DIRECTLY TO YOU IN YOUR PRESENT POSITION?
- SOMETHING SPECIAL

If the participants are not acquainted, I use the "buddy system" and ask them to interview the person sitting next to them, and I add one final item to the flip chart—"Something special about your buddy." This allows all the participants to relate something they are proud of—number of grandchildren, unique hobbies, and so on. Then each person introduces his or her buddy to the group.

As we begin the introductions, I have someone in the room keep a total of the number of years in management and the number of direct subordinates; I include myself in the introductions. After everyone has been introduced, my assistant will report that in the room there is a total of, say, 291 years of management experience; I write that figure boldly on the chart.

The following remarks have a profound impact on validating the students:

> "I want to promise this group at the outset that I will not teach you anything new. Did you know that every lesson that's ever been learned in dealing with people has already been learned in our aggregate 291 years of management experience? Every major mistake that's ever been made in management has already been made in the total experience of this group. In fact, I've made half of all these mistakes myself with no help from you! You see, the hard lessons we learn in management and human relations are somewhat like stepping on a rake. Once we've stepped on a rake, we tend not to step on that same rake again; that lesson now becomes part of our core of experience—a very valuable part.
>
> As a group, we've learned a lot of lessons—stepped on a lot of rakes. But not every person has learned every lesson. Joe, here, has valuable lessons that are different from those lessons Mary has learned.
>
> My wife, Liz, is a third-grade school teacher. When she goes to class, the body of knowledge lies in the teacher; she shares that knowledge with her students. In contrast, when I conduct a management seminar, the main body of knowledge is in the students. Yes, I bring my core of experience, but the real value is in the aggregate experience of you—the participants. One of the greatest benefits in such a setting is that when Mary shares an experience with Joe and with the rest of the class, she helps Joe, but she hasn't lost anything herself. In sharing tangible property, if I share my book with you, you have it, and I lose it. However, when sharing ideas and experiences, you don't lose them. That's a true win-win."

The psychological reaction to this introduction technique is usually the following set of positive realizations by the students:

1) The teacher and my fellow participants respect me and my knowledge and experiences.

2) I feel an obligation to participate actively in the discussion.
3) I have a valuable opportunity to learn a great deal of important information in a brief period of time.
4) I feel a personal responsibility for the overall success of this training session.
5) I feel good about myself and feel fortunate to be attending this seminar.

It's almost amusing when you witness the change in nonverbal messages. Before the introductions, many people sit back from the table, arms folded, ignoring the course materials, looking at their watches. After the introductions, they are sitting up close to the table, pencils out, smiling, and raring to go!

In transactional analysis jargon, we could say they entered the session in a state of "I'm not OK, you're not OK" — the introductions create an "I'm OK, you're OK" mindset. That's fertile ground for planting ideas.

The total number of subordinates reporting to the group is written on the chart next. Let's assume the total was 135. My next remarks are designed to motivate each participant to pay attention, take notes, listen carefully, and learn as much as possible.

> "We have 135 people looking to us daily for leadership, guidance, motivation, inspiration—we are very important to those 135 people. However, they are actually more important than we. They represent the 'leadership footprint' in this room."

There is one other psychological switch we must close before adults will truly buy in to a management training situation. In almost every management seminar I conduct, during a break, someone invariably says to me: "I sure wish my boss could be here. I never realized how badly he needed this training. I don't feel I need this, but I'd *pay* to get my boss to attend this session."

I'm sure you have experienced the same feelings; I have many times. It's important for us to understand why this reaction occurs and the dangers inherent in it.

First, we tend to externalize leadership instead of internalizing it. Since leadership exists in the minds of the followers, when we think of leadership, we naturally visualize leaders we observe, such as our bosses.

In our seminar, we discuss good leader behavior—we create a perfect leadership role model. Unfortunately, all of our bosses are flawed—just as we are.

As I paint this perfect picture, the participants are mentally comparing what I am describing with what they observe on the job. Sometimes, the longer they listen, the madder they get. The greatest risk of this phenomenon is that the participants could develop intense dissatisfaction for their boss and the organization. Not much learning takes place in such an environment. A good trainer will deal with this situation soon so that the participants don't "lock out" and fail to learn.

I usually discuss this phenomenon openly and conclude with, "...I'm sure you realize that your boss is flawed—just as each of us is flawed. Nobody is the perfect leader. But, the people we want to serve today are the 135 subordinates who see us as their leader.

"They will be the benefactors or victims of our skills or flaws. Today is *your* opportunity to improve *your* skills. Take notes in the first person—when I say 'good leaders should...,' you write 'I should...' This is *your* seminar. You'll miss a great opportunity to become a better leader if you sit here all day and pout over the flaws of your boss."

I face a little risk of alienating some participants, but I do it in good humor. Over the years, several participants have told me later, "I needed that."

TELL, SHOW, DO, OBSERVE, AND GIVE FEEDBACK

For years we've heard of the school of hard knocks, trial and error, and that rugged crucible which produces some of our most street-wise managers—"Sidewalk University." There seems to be a subtle pride when managers state, "I've learned how to supervise and train people by doing it." The mere fact that you haven't been fired, sued, or filed bankruptcy is taken as validation that you know how to train people. Some people measure excellence as the absence of failure. That's a rotten yardstick when you have the opportunity to grow, polish, hone, yes, even inspire people to strive for the rarefied air on the summit of performance instead of mushing along with the masses in the cracks and crevices of mediocrity.

I find it very difficult to let clients know their training programs are marginal—2 on a scale of 1 to 10 when they think they are a 2 on a scale of 1 to 3. Once they learn what real, high-impact training is all about, they strive to develop their programs to a perfect 10.

I want to share with you the concept, skills, and techniques of a top-flight training program; the pieces of the puzzle appear simple at first glance, but they all interact to produce a synergism that will have a profound, positive, long-term impact on your organization. Howard F. Shout's excellent book, *Start Supervising*, says it very succinctly; I'll elaborate on his ideas.[10]

The first and most important step in the training process is to select and train the trainer. Your trainers must be acknowledged experts in the subject matter. They should be confident but not arrogant; they should not only have the skills in question but they should also have a sincere desire to share those skills.

It's not surprising that the best training programs have the best people. Staff your training department with the type of people you want to clone because their talents, attitudes, and abilities will form the backbone of the next generation of your organization. Shout's book has several suggestions on selecting trainers. After you've honored your best employees by selecting them as trainers, take them through one of the excellent "train-the-trainer" programs on the market.

When I've selected one of my best employees to be a trainer, I interview him or her and *sell* the importance of this new role. These words seem to work: "I've selected you as a trainer because I want the next generation to be as good as you are. Did you ever think that, when you retire, the work skills you've mastered are of very little value on the golf course? I want you to leave your skills behind in the work of your students. When you think about it, your preparing the new employees properly will help this firm compete and profit well in the future. In fact, the people you train today are going to allow us to pay your retirement check in the years to come."

There are five basic steps in any effective training program. Most managers can recite the steps; I'd like to tell you why the steps are important and point out a few pitfalls awaiting the unwary trainer.

STEP 1—Break each job into its smaller sub-tasks and plan your training at the task level. You must first *tell* the employee the who, what, where, how, and why of the task. The term "tell" indicates one-way communication—Pitfall number one. I mean you have to communicate with employees in terms they understand. If employees are new to the organization, you've got to start your training in general language. You now have to teach them the language of the company as well as the details of the task.

STEP 2—*Show* the trainee the task performed properly. It's preferable for the trainee and trainer to sit side-by-side so the explanations of directions (left and right) are not reversed by sitting on opposite sides of a table. I strongly recommend the trainer be able to personally demonstrate the task; it does wonders for your credibility and personal power. Truly great instructors will practice "off stage"; they value the trainee's respect.

Another pitfall is the aside comment, "It's really simple; there's actually nothing to it." The trainer is telling the truth—it is simple after having done it hundreds of times; I'm sure the trainer makes that remark in an effort to reduce the trainee's apprehension. However, the statement may be *false* as it relates to a new employee who has never done the task before. Now, if the trainee experiences the normal clumsiness, he or she becomes even more embarrassed since the task was described as "really simple." Solution: Don't

94

make comments that set unrealistic expectations for the trainee. Be honest; acknowledge the basic truth that almost everything is complicated to a rookie. Most skilled employees psychologically suppress the memories of their early days when the job was complicated, and their success rate and self-esteem were low. Good trainers remember their thoughts, feelings, and uncertainties on "day one," even if it was many years ago.

STEP 3—Let the trainee actually *do* the task. It may be helpful for the trainee to tell the trainer what he or she intends to do just before doing it. This allows the trainer to prevent those crucial little goofs when the student's self-esteem is most fragile. Guide the trainee into doing the task correctly the *first* time. Sometimes you can ask the trainee to accomplish it at half speed so you can watch it more closely. This is a great morale booster, particularly when the trainee couldn't do it at normal speed anyhow; speed comes with confidence and proficiency. Let him or her practice that task a few times until he or she feels comfortable doing it. Another technique I've used to help the trainee master the skill when he or she understands the task but lacks confidence: I'll have the trainee assume the role of instructor and teach me the skill. This role reversal tends to boost self-esteem and confidence.

STEP 4—*Observe* the trainee closely, study his or her face and eyes for non-verbal signs of confusion and nervousness. Mask your own non-verbal messages; don't appear nervous; the trainee will detect and amplify your nervousness. Look closely for the "good news"; what did he or she do right? Reinforce the successes first and frequently. Instead of saying, "Most of that was OK, but you had problems with the last part," try, "That was excellent for a first time; practice it a few more times to smooth out the rough spots." I can't give you a script for being a good trainer, but I can encourage you to exhibit a mature, supportive, and professional attitude.

STEP 5—Provide *feedback*. Give the trainee the credit for success, regardless of how minute. But assume a lion's share of the blame if he or she errs. A far wiser one than I said, "If the student hasn't learned, then the teacher hasn't taught." I learned the following phrase from one of the greatest teachers I've known. When I would stumble, he would say: "I don't think I explained that very well; let me try again." That always helped my learning more than verbal and non-verbal messages that shouted, "This guy is not very bright."

DOCUMENT ALL TRAINING

One of the major shortcomings I've seen in training programs is the failure to properly document the training. Oh, I can see you wince now. Documentation spells paperwork. Most busy people abhor additional paperwork; I know I do.

But it's also true that we do not abhor things we value. For example, most folks don't mind getting letters of commendation. Pages upon pages of verbosity which describe our charm, intelligence, and exceptional professionalism have never been termed "just more damn paperwork." But in truth, that's exactly what it is. The only difference is the perceived value we place upon it.

The trick to getting proper documentation for the fine training that's been accomplished is to increase its value to you and your organization. Brace yourself! You're about to be sold the value of proper training documentation (that is, paperwork).

At the end of this appendix, you'll find the three forms which make up all effective training systems. **Exhibit A-1** is a sample position description (PD) of an administrative secretary; notice in section B that there is one primary duty and there are two secondary duties.

Exhibit A-2 is a Job Performance Standard (JPS) for the position stated in A-1. Please note that the three major duties in A-1 are also listed in A-2, but now we know what "manage properly," "effectively support," and "effectively route" actually mean in specific terms.

Exhibit A-3 is the Job Training Standard (JTS) for someone assuming the position of administrative secretary. Through an effective training program, one-by-one the specific skills and abilities related to each task will be
96

Non-Exempt Position Description

Salary Grade: _____

Hay Points: _____

New: _____

Functional Position Title: __Administrative Secretary__ Job #: _____ Rev.: _____

Division: __XYZ Corporation__ Prepared By: __Susan White__

Department: __Real Estate__ Approved By: _____ Date: _____

Reports To: (Title) _____ Reviewed By: _____ Date: _____

A. Position Summary:

In coordination with VP Real Estate is responsible for all administrative matters pertaining to resale of foreclosed properties.

B. Description of Specific Responsibilities: (List duties in order of importance.) Continue on attachment if necessary.

Principal Duties and Responsibilities	% Time Spent
I. Primary	
Manages the documentation flow for resale of foreclosed property.	75%
II. Secondary	
To assist the Executive Secretary in all general secretarial duties.	10%
To provide assistance to other employees within the department and act as a contact for employees outside the department in providing general information.	15%

This position description includes representative duties which may not be a complete list of all duties required for the position.

500.00.015 6/85

A-1

Job Performance Standard

Functional Position Title: __Administrative Secretary__

Department: __Real Estate__   Prepared By: __Susan White__

Date: __June 11, 1991__   Approved By: _____

Standards for Principal Duties and Responsibilities. (Ref. Non-Exempt Position Description, Section B and Job Training Standard, Section VI)

1. Manage properly the documentation for resale of foreclosed property.

   A. Resales will be booked within two working days of receipt.

   B. Vacant property files will be entered into the system within three working days.

   C. Non-monetary items will have no more than a 1% error rate.

   D. Legal and/or monetary items will have 100% accuracy.

   E. Utility bills be processed within two working days.

   F. Sales messages will be transmitted accurately on same day received.

   G. Upon request from customer for title, initial action will be taken within five working days.

   H. Within six weeks of receipt of documentation from customer, transaction will be completed.

   I. End of month reports should be completed within two working days after receipt of accounting reports.

2. Effectively support the Executive Secretary.

   A. Within 24 hours of request, assistance will be initiated.

3. Effectively route inquiries to the proper offices for assistance.

   A. Demonstrate a willingness to accurately handle inquiries and route accordingly.

A-2

mastered by the trainee to the satisfaction of the trainer. When that occurs, they jointly date and initial that item in the JTS. Bear in mind that this brief ritual takes place *after* the trainee has actually demonstrated the skill, never before.

In some immature organizations, there may be a tendency to "pencil whip" the training record. This is devastating for several reasons. First, if you fake the documentation, then no one really knows what the facts are concerning the true abilities of the employee. Second, the employee loses respect for the trainer and the organization. Finally, if the practice is wide-spread, the courts may hold the trainer and the organization liable if an employee is injured or killed as a result of improper training. Bottom line— never, never play fast and loose with training records. I assure you, such unprofessional practices will put you, your employees, and your organization on a one-way trip to "lose-lose land."

But what are the benefits to be gained from proper, honest documentation? There are many; here are only a few:

1) The ritual of jointly documenting the successes at the task level is measurable, visible, positive reinforcement for both the trainer and the trainee. It's easier for both parties to reach for the next rung on the ladder if they are standing, together, on a platform of success.

2) This approach reduces the chances of some tasks being over-looked during the training program; it provides a much tighter overall system.

3) When a trainee initials the task entry, he or she is accepting responsibility and accountability for performing that task prop-erly on the job. This crucial fact is best developed by two brief scenarios.

Case #1: Joe is trained through incidental, informal, on-the-job training. He was told to work with Jack for a few weeks.

Job Training Standard (JTS)

Functional Position Title   Administrative Secretary

Employee's Name   *Jane R. Doe*   Date hired/transferred   *July 7, 1991*

Supervisor's Name   *Sue Jones*

Trainer's Name   *Beth L. Smith*

Department   Real Estate   JTS Approved By   *Charles C Carpenter*

Optimum Training Period   Three (3) weeks

Estimated Completion Date   *July 28, 1991*

Actual Completion Date   *August 11, 1991 (5 days sick leave)*

Probation Dates   *July 7, 1991*   To   *October 7, 1991*

Immediately after administrative in-processing is completed, formal employee orientation/training begins. If employee is transferred from another department, complete this JTS for only those new duties associated with the new position.

*Conducted by Corporate Services

		Date Completed	Trainer Initials	Trainee Initials
* I.	Industry orientation	*Jul 8*	*BJS*	*DRE*
*II.	Corporation orientation	*Jul 8*	*BJS*	*DRL*
III.	Department orientation by Supervisor			
	A. Welcome/Depart. Introductions	*Jul 8*	*BJS*	*DRE*
	B. Depart. function within the company	*Jul 9*	*BJS*	*DR*
	C. Depart. layout and facilities	*Jul 9*	*BJS*	*DR*
	D. Depart. procedures	*Jul 9*	*BJS*	*DR*
	1. Emergency (fire, tornado, illness, etc.)	*Jul 9*	*BJS*	*DR*
	2. Safety/Housekeeping	*Jul 9*	*BJS*	*DR*
	3. Dress Code	*Jul 9*	*BJS*	*DR*
	4. Department telephone codes	*Jul 9*	*BJS*	*DR*

VI. **Demonstrates ability to:**

	Date Completed	Trainer Initials	Trainee Initials
1. Manage properly the documentation for resale of foreclosed property.	Jul 23	BJS	JRL
2. Effectively support the executive secretary.	Aug 7	BJS	JRL
3. Effectively route inquiries to the proper offices for assistance.	Aug 11	BJS	JRL
4.			
5.			
6.			

Remarks: Please date and sign all entries. Although Jane progressed satisfactor she was absent July 28 – August 1, due to the flu. Therefore, her training period was extended to compensate for her absence.

Beth L. Smith
August 11, 1991

Department Review/Approval   Signature: Elizabeth J Stephens   Date Aug 13, 1991

Corporate Review/Approval   Signature: Charles Coulter   Date Aug 15, 1991

Allow me a brief insert here to help make what follows more important. I'm sure you realize that most positions have what I term "job cycle." This is the time period when all normal tasks within the job occur at least once. For example, there are tasks my administrative assistant accomplishes many times daily—answers phones, types, files, and so on. However, there are a few tasks she accomplishes only once each year—taxes. So it actually takes an entire year to experience all tasks within her job—her job cycle is twelve months. It's not reasonable to train an administrative assistant for twelve months, but we need an organized system to provide some familiarity with *all* the tasks before the employee is shoved into deep water all alone. Solution: My administrative assistant's Job Training Standard has the task entry "Prepare financial reports for annual taxes." Before my last administrative assistant moved to Texas, she spent an afternoon with my current administrative assistant discussing the why's and wherefore's of that important but infrequently performed task. Yes, they both initialled the JTS.

Now back to Case #1 and the trials and tribulations of Joe, a new employee. After a few days, Joe has become comfortable with most of the tasks that have cycled several times during his time with Jack. Jack is falling behind his normal workload, so he's encouraged to tell his boss that Joe is doing OK and is ready to do his job. As a result of Jack's report and the press of business, Joe is declared "trained" and sent to work, more-or-less unsupervised; so far—so good.

One month later, during one of Joe's shifts, an expensive piece of equipment overheats and catches fire, destroying it and part of a building; luckily Joe and his co-workers were unhurt. An investigation reveals the machine had run out of oil. Joe was charged with negligence and fired.

Now the plot thickens like an Irish stew. Joe contacts the American Civil Liberties Union (ACLU) claiming he was wrongly discharged. He swears he was never told he needed to monitor the oil level in that machine—"I thought it was a sealed unit." The ACLU lawyers file a lawsuit against Joe's former employer.

Let's skip the gory details. Despite the folklore about being innocent until proven guilty, here's what actually happens as our story unfolds. Joe doesn't have to prove he *wasn't* trained; the company has to prove that he *was*! Since the company did not bother to document whatever training Joe received, the absence of any meaningful records strengthens Joe's position and puts the company in a dangerous position.

When the smoke clears here's what you can expect:

1) The court will order Joe reinstated with back pay.
2) The company may have already hired a replacement for Joe; what do they do with him when Joe returns?
3) The company will pay attorneys' fees, court costs, and possibly, punitive damages.
4) The company must also pay for the new machine and repairs to the building.
5) Next year, their insurance rates will go up drastically.
6) They must now establish a proper training program with documentation. Better late than never.
7) Joe's employment situation will be subtly monitored by the ACLU to be sure he suffers no retribution. If Joe happens to have questionable work habits, he could give his supervisor a real headache and the company would have to convince the courts that their disciplinary actions were due to his present poor performance and not to retribution.

I could probably dredge up a few more "hits" for the company, but I think I've made my point.

Now let's present Case #2, and see if proper training documentation is of value when compared to the disaster in Case #1. When Joe arrives he is assigned to Jack, a seasoned employee who has been trained and is responsible for orienting new employees. During the next few weeks, Joe and Jack work through the Job Training Standard. When they get to the task of changing the oil in that machine, Jack arranges to let Joe visit another department which had scheduled an oil change on one of their machines; Joe helps do it. When he returns to Jack, they initial that entry in his Job Training Standard.

Our scenario could take one of two directions here. In all probability, Joe will change the oil in his machine at the proper time and everyone will live happily ever after. Or he may screw up and fail to do so, resulting in the aforementioned fire, damage, and discharge.

However, if Joe goes to the ACLU, the lawyers will find during the discovery proceeding that Joe initialled that he knew the proper procedures relating to the machine.

The output of such documentation will be:

1) No lawsuit.
2) Joe stays fired.
3) A strong message is sent to employees who are properly trained and then become negligent.
4) The company's losses are limited to replacing the equipment, repairing the building, and paying higher insurance premiums.

It's time to take a hard look at the bottom-line value of a meaningful training program with proper documentation in these two situations. If we estimate the court costs, fines, back-pay, and lost productivity in Case #1, we can began to appreciate the value of that "damned training paperwork" in Case #2.

You may accuse me of being a bit melodramatic, of going beyond the bounds of realism. Not guilty; I've actually seen similar cases that would make this story pale by comparison. I hope, however, that you are now as convinced as I am that we don't train and document because we need to cover our back-sides from lawyers —we do so because it's just plain good business.

WHEN IS IT "GOOD ENOUGH"?

While conducting research in the Air War College, I came upon a unique concept described in E. Frank Harrison's book, *The Managerial Decision Making Process.*[11] "Satisficing is the process of rationally comparing the qualitative difference between the values of the optimal solution with benefits and values associated with a 'satisfactory' solution, provided it is 'good enough.'" Certainly, an optimal solution has many obvious advantages, but there are some less obvious developmental benefits which flow from letting an employee "get in the game" with a satisfactory solution.

On a scale of 1 to 10, an experienced employee might be able to perform a particular task at a ten level of competence. A trainee might only be able to perform at a seven level. Will the seven get the job done adequately? If it will, you may be well advised to take it with thanks.

Sure, the seasoned employee can do the job better; you knew that. And, if seasoned employees could handle every company requirement, and you expected no growth or change, no retirements or resignations, you would not need a training program. But heaven hasn't come to the workplace, and managers still have to get the job done with the resources they have. And sometimes the best way to accomplish that feat is to accept less than a ten. That's one of the best ways to eventually get the trainee to produce at a ten level of competence.

There's a story about a young executive who made a bad decision that cost the company $50,000. Realizing the gross error, the dejected manager went to the CEO, admitted the mistake and concluded the confession with, "Well, I guess I'm going to be fired, and I can't say I blame you."

"I can't fire you now!" the CEO yelled. "We have just spent $50,000 on your professional development!"

That example is a little extreme. The point is: Keep in touch so development lessons don't cost $50,000 each. Establish acceptable levels of performance, measure the marginal value—the qualitative difference—between the trainee's seven and a ten, and evaluate what you will gain in development and commitment if you take the seven. If there is a positive flow between that analysis and the results, take it.

If you require the ten because it is available, and you lose the commitment of your subordinate, you haven't really gained in the developmental sense. You've missed a chance to develop the individual one more step if you don't give him or her a chance to get in there and take a swing at the ball.

Effective managers use their coaching skills to show a subordinate how their seven becomes an eight and the eight becomes a nine. If you can make that happen, your organization has gained. However, you must be sensitive to the lowest acceptable level of performance; a six won't do if seven is the floor.

GOOD TRAINING IS MOTIVATIONAL

I've been asked by managers on four continents, "How can I motivate my employees?" The straight answer is, "You can't."

True motivation is self-motivation; the term literally means "to move from within." Of course, if you have enough whips and chains, you can drag your employees around for eight hours, but that's not motivation—that's power! One sure-fire thing I've found that tends to get people motivated is involving them in high-impact training in skills they value.

In 1971, I attended the United States Air Force Jungle Survival School at Clark Air Base in the Philippines. My next assignment was to fly 137 combat missions over the jungles of Laos. From high in my OV-10 Bronco airplane, the dense, green rain forest was beautiful; on the jungle floor were tigers, snakes, and enemy soldiers bent on shooting me down. You can't imagine the level of motivation among the students in jungle survival school.

Granted, most jobs in industry and business aren't as dangerous, but the trick is to relate the student's mastery of the skills to their achieving some goal *they* value. Too often the instructors relate the skills only to benefits that flow to the organization or the boss. These are important and should be mentioned, but don't forget to answer the question that's burning at gut level for every student—"What's in it for me?"

GOOD LEADERSHIP SKILLS ARE LEARNED

Many people think leadership is Common Sense 101, that such skills come with living. Wrong. Leaders are not born knowing how to influence the actions of others.

Leadership requires a set of skills just as brain surgery and computer operation require certain abilities. I think that, many times, leadership and management are more complicated than the highly technical professions; the leader's job is certainly becoming more complex every day!

There are many good managers and leaders out there doing their thing; they know their profession. Unfortunately, there are many more who don't. This situation has developed through natural changes in organizations. For example, an engineer does a good job and is promoted to department head; the top salesperson becomes sales manager. What they often fail to realize is that they are no longer an engineer or a salesperson; they are managers. And they are starting at the bottom of a new career field; they have to learn a new profession.

They have moved from a self-centered, task-oriented role to one that is other-person-centered and behavior-oriented. What they do now will affect everyone below them in their organization. Their responsibility has shifted from satisfactory completion of a narrowly defined task to a function that shifts with the situational sands. And they must now influence individuals or a group in efforts toward achievement of their common organization's goals. They have become leaders. Leaders need training in order to function effectively, and organizations need effective leaders in order to survive.

NOTES ON APPENDIX

10. Shout, Howard F. *Start Supervising*. Washington, DC. The Bureau of National Affairs, Inc. 1984.

11. Harrison, E. Frank. *The Managerial Decision-Making Process*. Boston, Massachusetts. Houghton Mifflin Company. 1975.